WHAT'S BEING SAID ABOUT The Confederate Challenge:

"... a delight to historians and the general public ... detailed information ... a starting point for discussions ... unashamedly pro-Southern and rightfully so ... "
John McGlone, Editor
Journal of Confederate History

"This book is *must reading* ... a comprehensive portrait of the triumphs and tragedies of the Southern Civil War experience."
Prof. Edward C. Smith
The American University
Washington, D.C.

"... exciting new work ... a fresh educational approach ... the book's ultimate contribution will be achieved when the reader discovers a significant fact that inspires ... additional investigation ... "
Rick Griffin, Commander
Army of Northern Virginia Dept.
Sons of Confederate Veterans

"The author's love of the period is reflected in this delightful collection of little known facts."

John Edward Hurley
Confederate Memorial Hall
Washington, D.C.

Illustrated by Jeffery N. Prechtel

THE CONFEDERATE CHALLENGE

1,001 Questions and Answers about the War of the Rebellion

THE CONFEDERATE CHALLENGE

1,001 Questions and Answers about the War of the Rebellion

John M. Hightower

Foreword by James J. Cooke

Rockbridge Publishing Company
Natural Bridge Station, Virginia

Published by

Rockbridge Publishing Company
Post Office Box 70
Natural Bridge Station, VA 24579
Telephone (703) 291-1063
Facsimile (703) 291-1346

Copyright 1992 by John M. Hightower
All rights reserved
Printed in the United States of America

Illustrated by Jeffery N. Prechtel

Library of Congress Cataloging-in-Publication Data

Hightower, John M., 1940-
    The Confederate challenge : 1,001 questions and answers about the War of the Rebellion / John M. Hightower; foreword by James J. Cooke. — 1st ed.
      p. cm.
    Includes bibliographical references and index.
    ISBN 0-9623572-6-X
    1. United States--History--Civil War, 1861-1865--Miscellanea.
I. Title.
E468.9.H6   1992
973.7--dc20   92-34353
                                                                            CIP

10 9 8 7 6 5 4 3 2 1
First Edition

To Dolores

Contents

Searching for Real Rebels *by James J. Cooke* vii
A Challenge Accepted ix

QUESTIONS   1-94

Southern Heroes
Jefferson Davis 1
Robert E. Lee 2
Stonewall Jackson 3
Officers and Gentlemen 4
Southern Women 12
Patriots All 16
Notable Quotes 18

In the Ranks
Units 25
Uniforms and Equipment 28
Flags, Symbols and Decorations 31
In Camp 34
Combat and Tactics 35
Weapons 39
Forts, Prisons and Hospitals 46

Total War
War in the East 51
War in the West 57
War at Sea 61
War on Rails 66
Strategy 68
Geography 71

The Cause
    Politics and Government 77
    The Homefront 84
    Music, Words and Images............................ 87
    After Appomattox 91

ANSWERS   **95-119**

Select Bibliography.. 121
Index... 123
About the Author 139

Searching for Real Rebels

More than 130 years have passed since the end of the War, yet interest in the great American conflict remains strong. Every year dozens of new books are snapped up by a public eager and willing to learn more about those four turbulent and bloody years. There is a sense that a profound thing happened to Americans from 1861 to 1865, that the men who marched away, fought, bled and died participated in a singular moment in history, in a war more real to us than any fought before it.

For the first time, improved techniques of photography brought the War home. The haunting eyes of a Georgia boy slain at Malvern Hill, the contorted bodies of bloating Federal dead at Gettysburg and the dignity of the sorrowing Lee are accepted as real life flesh and blood, not an artist's interpretation. Time loses its meaning and years evaporate as these images reach from the page and seize the viewer. Today we can still see the true face of the War.

Nobel prize winner William Faulkner knew that in the heart of every Southern boy there is that small space that transports him to Gettysburg on July 3, 1863. He knew that for Southerners, the War will never be quite finished. No other portion of the United States has ever suffered such devastation, such defeat, such occupation as Old Dixie.

Henry W. Grady of Atlanta called out to put the past to rest, but this history cannot be discarded. The monuments at Shiloh, the Warren County court house in Vicksburg, the White House of the Confederacy in Richmond and that saddest of all places, the McLean house at Appomattox, all testify to a nation that is no more. Sacred family relics, like the letter of Jeremiah Gage of the University Grays of the 11th Mississippi, stained with his dying blood, keep this history alive today.

Almost every Southern family has a War story: how Auntie

saved the silver from Sherman's bummers, or how Grandfather enlisted at age 14. As might be expected in such turbulent times, tall tales and stories also cropped up. Misconceptions flourished and endured!

And therein lies the value of this book. At a time when a national news magazine reports that a frightening percentage of American high school students cannot even place the War in the proper century, it is good to have a handy compendium of 1,001 facts about the War and the South, facts that encompass the vastness of the Confederate experience, from the obvious to the obscure. It is more than a trivia game book — a war which cost so much in human treasure can never be trivialized.

Television's presentation of the facts, personalities and events of the American Civil War, though generous in the amount of air time, is weighed in terms of ratings. (Surely not all Southern girls were beautiful, aristocratic belles with laughable accents. Where are the sturdy, supportive wives and daughters of the yeoman farmer privates and corporals who carried the Confederacy on the tips of their bayonets?)

The Confederate Challenge, then, is a book of facts, 1,001 of them, that answers questions free of interpretation and revisionism. This small book, by the way, is decidedly Southern — no blue-coat sympathy here. Facts about the real rebels, the men and women who tried to make a new nation, are to be found within these pages. This book will amuse, to be sure, but it will also educate those who seek the plain facts of history.

JAMES J. COOKE

University of Mississippi

A Challenge Accepted

The Confederate Challenge was born of a desire to know a little about a great deal. In attempting to reach that august goal I admit some small measure of success, but the hunger still remains.

I am indebted to Gilbert Strosnider, a fellow member of the Sons of Confederate Veterans, who labored over many of these questions and answers. His tenacity in ferreting out interesting facts and little known occurrences was indeed laudable.

This project would never have reached completion without the aid of my helpmate and wife, Dolores, who translated the holographic questions and answers and committed them to disc.

Tom Lewis and John Sours of the Civil War Society encouraged the endeavor and answered many questions when conflicting sources appeared. Their advice and opinions are gratefully reflected herein.

Encouragement from compatriots in the Sons of Confederate Veterans was heartening. Rick Griffin, Commander of the Army of Northern Virginia, was inspirational, as were Dave Melton, Ken Beauchamp, Harold Woodward, Jr., and many others. Both a compatriot and a learned professor, Jim Cooke of the University of Mississippi listened attentively and generously shared his insight and expertise on the subject.

John Edward Hurley of Confederate Memorial Hall, Washington, D.C., quietly suggested valuable areas of interest that might be explored. Professor Ed Smith of American University pointed with considerable pride to the contributions and accomplishments of black patriots who fought for the South and served the Cause on the homefront as well.

Kathie Tennery's editorial and research skills are finely honed, and her direction and great patience are deeply appreciated.

Part of the challenge in collecting these facts was separating them from historical fiction. Accuracy was the watchword in gleaning the grain from the chaff, but with such a complex body of material, there is little doubt that errors will surface. Corrections received with recognized authority will be cheerfully acknowledged and included in subsequent editions.

What C.P. Snow said about Red China many years ago can be applied equally well to the War for Southern Independence: "There are no experts, only varying degrees of ignorance." It is hoped this work will educate, but it is designed for fun and stimulation, too. There are no hard questions if the answers are known.

John M. Hightower
Berryville, Virginia
August 1992

"Wherever there is a Southern heart to beat with indignation at Southern wrongs, there a Southern tongue may tell the story of their existence, and counsel their redress."

— *Robert Barnwell Rhett*

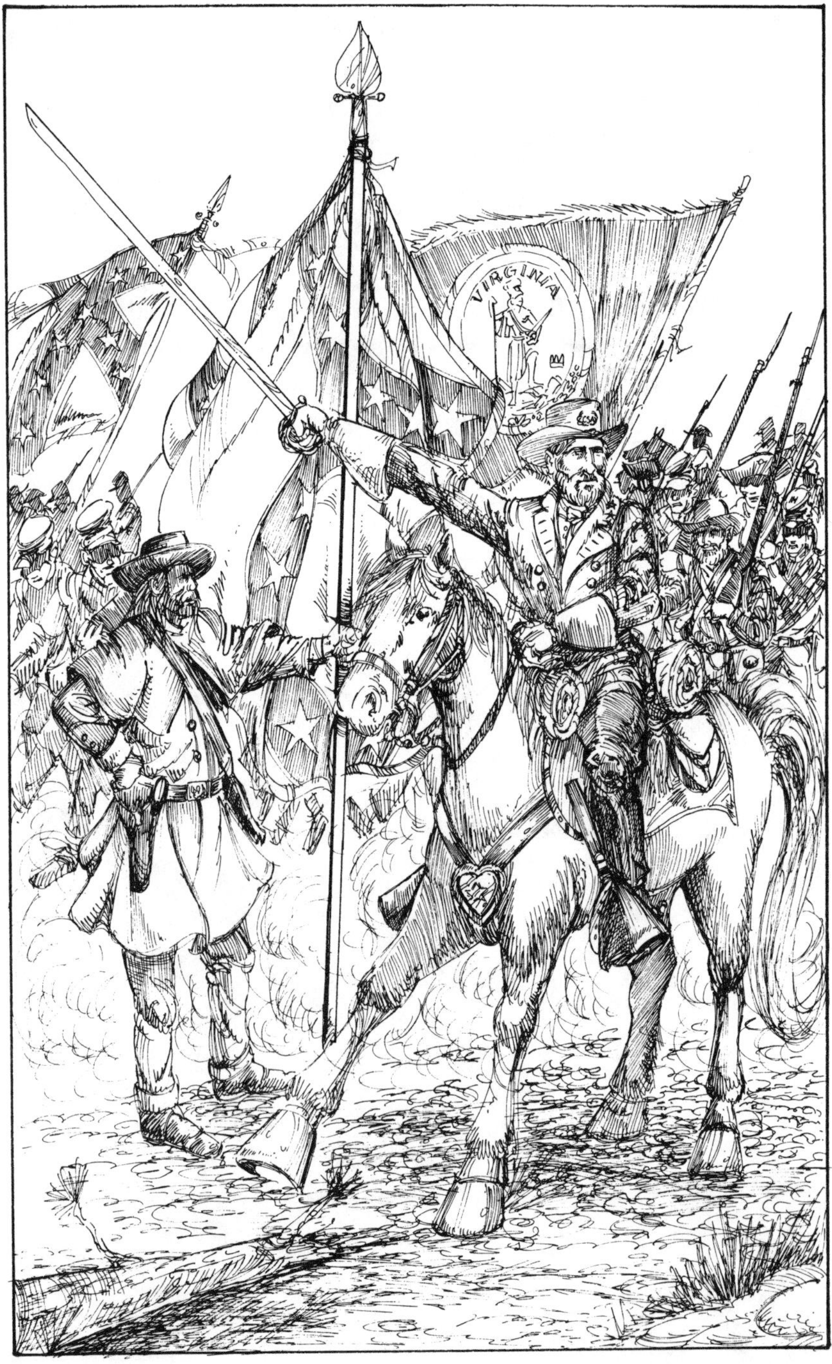
VIRGINIA

Southern Heroes

Jefferson Davis

1. In what year was President Davis's term of office to be concluded?

2. What was the amount of the reward offered by the Yankees for the capture of Jefferson Davis?

3. Where did Jefferson Davis see action in the Mexican War?

4. President Davis issued an order that this Yankee general was to be shot on sight by any Southern patriot.

5. Near what Mississippi town was Jefferson Davis living when he was elected president of the provisional government?

6. Name the five-year-old son of Jefferson Davis who fell to his death in Richmond.

7. Jefferson Davis predicted the North would do this to history if they won the war.

8. President Davis's inaugural ball was held here in Montgomery, Alabama.

9. When was Jefferson Davis's citizenship restored by the U.S. Congress?

10. How many times did Jefferson Davis serve in the U.S. Senate?

11. Where was Jefferson Davis first buried?

12. What was Jefferson Davis's middle name?

13. For whom was Jefferson Davis named?

14. The first two months in Richmond, President Davis lived here while the White House was being renovated.

15. One of Jefferson Davis's final acts as a U.S. senator was to protest this military action to President Buchanan.

Robert E. Lee

16. Lee last served at this post prior to his resignation from the U.S. Army.

17. Lee's famous horse, Traveller, was earlier known by these two names.

18. A postwar Federal grand jury indicted Lee as a traitor, but this man had it quashed.

19. What was Lee's most pressing problem when he took over the Confederate army at Richmond?

20. Lee and Stonewall Jackson first met as superior and subordinate at Dabb's House, north of Richmond, on what date?

21. This Virginia battle is considered Lee's greatest tactical victory.

22. On what religious holiday did Lee surrender to Grant?

23. Where was Lee when he refused the command of the

U.S. Army?

24. After the War for Southern Independence this U.S. president invited Lee to the White House.

25. After the War, Lee said this Yankee general was the best Northern opponent he had faced.

26. What was the content of Lee's 1865 General Order No. 9?

27. Lee accepted his commission to lead Virginia troops on this date.

28. She was Lee's lesser-known war horse.

29. After the War, with whom did Lee "wander out in the mountains and enjoy sweet confidences?"

30. Lee offered to do this after the battle of Gettysburg.

Stonewall Jackson

31. In what clothing was Stonewall Jackson buried?

32. Stonewall Jackson commanded V.M.I. cadets at this Abolitionist's execution in Charles Town, (West) Virginia.

33. What nickname was given to Stonewall Jackson by the V.M.I. Cadets?

34. Stonewall Jackson tendered his resignation because of an action taken by this Southern statesman.

35. Where did Stonewall Jackson capture a record number of Yankees?

36. Which General Hill was related by marriage to Stonewall Jackson?

37. Where did Stonewall Jackson die?

38. Who was Stonewall Jackson's private cook?

39. After the War, this Southern hero lived in a house once occupied by Stonewall Jackson in Lexington, Virginia.

40. What protective garment was Stonewall Jackson wearing when he was shot at Chancellorsville?

41. This surgeon was Stonewall Jackson's medical director and his personal doctor.

42. In this Virginia battle, Stonewall Jackson found his edged weapon rusted in its scabbard.

Officers and Gentlemen

43. At West Point, he broke a plate on the head of fellow cadet Jubal Early.

44. This Confederate general lay in state long after he was buried.

45. This former U.S. vice-president ran for the U.S. presidency and later became a C.S.A. general.

46. Gen. John McCausland burned Chambersburg, Pennsylvania, in retaliation for this man's burning in the Valley of Virginia.

47. This pharmacist-turned-C.S.A.-general was born in Ireland.

48. He wept over his "poor orphans" after the Battle of Murfreesboro.

49. When this Confederate leader was killed near White's Tavern on August 16, 1864, the Yankees found a map of

the defenses of Richmond on him.

50. This Confederate general laid aside his Episcopal bishop's robe for a uniform.

51. Lee called him the "Old War Horse."

52. This U.S. Military Academy graduate and a C.S.A. general was the owner of the Tredegar Iron Works.

53. Yankee Lt. A. Willis Gould nearly killed this brigadier general of a Confederate cavalry unit.

54. Who was Stonewall Jackson's cartographer?

55. He waterproofed an empty beer keg and turned it into a torpedo used against Yankee ships.

56. He was Nathan Bedford Forrest's chief of artillery.

57. This Southern one-time general was reduced in rank to colonel.

58. His war-time marriage was conducted at St. Paul's church in Richmond, where three weeks later his funeral was held.

59. These two Southern generals fought a duel in Little Rock, Arkansas, in 1863.

60. This Southern general was shot in the throat and the bullet lodged in his right shoulder during the Battle of the Wilderness.

61. This prince was the only French alien to attain a high rank in the Confederate Army.

62. When Jefferson Davis had to replace Gen. Braxton Bragg, this general refused the command.

63. This Partisan Ranger's greatest value to the Cause was in distracting 30,000 Yankees from Lee's army.

64. After the Rebellion, these major generals C.S.A. became major generals U.S.A.

65. Lee removed him from command following the battle at Sayler's Creek.

66. What fraternal tie did Gen. P.G.T. Beauregard and Maj. Robert H. Anderson have?

67. A bullet hole in his hat kept him from drowning in his own blood during the Battle of Antietam.

68. This Southern general was wearing Masonic studs in his shirt when he fell mortally wounded at Gettysburg.

69. In the early days of the War, he commanded U.S. dragoons at Fort Manassas; he then resigned his commission to serve the Southern Cause and rose to the rank of brigadier general.

70. Gen. Beauregard was his artillery instructor at West Point and later faced him at Charleston.

71. This South Carolina patriot died in a fall from his horse when a stirrup broke.

72. Why did Maj. Gen. Winfield Scott Hancock, U.S.A., take charge of the personal effects of Brig. Gen. Lewis Armistead, C.S.A.?

73. He is mentioned more often in Lee's dispatches than any other Southern officer.

74. Who was the South's "fighting chaplain"?

75. This South Carolina general's father named him for a political movement.

76. This general fought in 63 battles and engagements without suffering a wound.

77. This Confederate general, a former commandant of cadets at West Point, was killed by a picket volley in his native Georgia.

78. What did John Singleton Mosby not do at the end of the War?

79. How many Southern generals died or received mortal wounds in battle?

80. Under what circumstances did most Southern generals

die?

81. Gen. J.E.B. Stuart's force of how many men rode around the aggressor's army of 115,000 and escaped nearly unscathed?

82. When Mosby captured Yankee Gen. Edwin Henry Stoughton asleep at Fairfax, how many men did the "Grey Ghost" have with him?

83. Prior to joining the Confederate Army, he was paymaster of the U.S. Army.

84. This cavalry officer captured 31,000 Yankees, had 29 horses shot out from under him, personally killed 30 of the aggressors and was under fire 179 times.

85. When the pro-Union state of Kentucky ordered his militia unit to turn in their arms, he shipped off rifle boxes filled with bricks.

86. Where was Gen. Albert Sidney Johnston killed?

87. In his role in the 1860 electoral college process, this future C.S.A. general announced the election of Abraham Lincoln.

88. His force of 3,000 Southerners hindered McClellan's progress in the Peninsular Campaign.

89. Gen. McClellan claimed a bloodless "victory" when this Confederate general repositioned his army closer to Richmond after the siege of Yorktown.

90. How many regular U.S. army officers had resigned their commissions to serve the South by the time of 1st Manassas?

91. Three separate funerals were held for this cavalry leader, in Abingdon and Richmond, Virginia, and in Lexington,

Kentucky.

92. He was President Davis's principle military advisor in the War's final battles.

93. Gen. Edmund Kirby Smith operated this military academy in antebellum times.

94. This Virginian was given the name "Swamp Fox of the Confederacy."

95. This Confederate leader was the superintendent of West Point for five days in January of 1861.

96. This Confederate brigadier general prisoner of war was hit in the head by a sword-wielding Yankee colonel and spent his remaining 47 years mentally disabled.

97. He made fun of Yankees in his prewar book on mathematics. ("A Yankee mixes a certain quantity of wooden nutmegs which cost him 1/4 cent apiece with a quantity of real nutmegs worth 4 cents . . . " etc.)

98. He was the first Confederate brigadier general to die from battle wounds.

99. Scarlet fever took the lives of his three children in Richmond in January 1862, causing his personality to become dour.

100. In what battle was Gen. Joseph E. Johnston wounded?

101. On the second invasion of Pennsylvania, this one-legged lieutenant general commanded the vanguard of the Confederate army.

102. This former U.S. president was the grandfather of Gen. George W. Randolph, C.S.A.

103. This Confederate general was mortally wounded at

Falling Waters; he died of his wounds at Bunker Hill, Virginia (now West Virginia).

104. This general was killed in the final defense of Petersburg.

105. Where was Brig. Gen. James E. Rains killed?

106. Gen. Joseph Johnston was severly wounded at Seven Pines but refused to leave the field until this personal item was recovered.

107. This Southern cavalry general was killed by Pennsylvania Bucktails while leading the 1st Maryland Infantry in a counter attack at Harrisonburg, Virginia, on June 6, 1862.

108. This Confederate general was fired upon by the Yankee artillery at Sharpsburg because from a distance he looked like General Lee.

109. Ordered to Vicksburg to lead cavalry, he instead commanded infantry there.

110. He designed the defensive fortifications at Charleston.

111. Brig. Gen. Lloyd Tilghman was killed in this Mississippi battle on May 16, 1863.

112. This Confederate cavalryman properly anticipated what the enemy cavalry was doing in 1862 because he had debated his father-in-law, Gen. Philip St. George Cooke, U.S.A., on the fine points of cavalry usage.

113. This Texan served Gen. John D. Imboden as his battery commander in 1863-1864.

114. Hard fighting for the Cause earned this general his nickname.

115. He was mortally wounded while directing Southern

batteries at Cedar Mountain.

116. This officer's father was commander at Fort McHenry during the bombardment in the War of 1812.

117. He was often referred to as "Jeff Davis's pet."

118. Despite a clean uniform and fresh white gloves, Gen. Joseph Johnston aided his men in wresting one of these from the mud.

119. Following the death of this Stonewall Brigade acting commander, the brigade was reduced to regimental strength.

120. How many Southerners attained brigadier general rank or higher?

121. How many Confederate generals graduated from West Point?

122. What percent of the 239 regular U.S. Army officers resigned their commissions to serve the Cause?

123. He rose from private to full colonel in the Va. cavalry.

124. Gen. J.E.B. Stuart tweaked this Yankee via telegraph; he complained about the condition of captured Federal mules.

125. This was Gen. Jubal Early's favorite whiskey.

126. He slept in Gen. William T. Sherman's captured bed at Shiloh.

127. He was the only native-born Texan to be made a Confederate general.

128. What was the highest rank a Confederate general could achieve?

129. This Southern general was murdered in Spring Hill, Tennessee, by a jealous husband.

130. He was the father of Gen. Richard Taylor, C.S.A., of Louisiana.

131. Confederate cartographer Maj. Jedediah Hotchkiss was from this Northern city.

132. Where was Gen. John C. Pemberton born?

133. This engineer captain was killed by the same volley that wounded Stonewall Jackson at Chancellorsville.

134. This Marylander was both an admiral and a general in the service of the Confederacy.

135. This Northerner by birth designed the Cape Fear defense system.

136. This Southern officer observed the fighting at Gaines's Mill from a balloon.

137. This Virginia cavalry leader's daring exploits included a clandestine intelligence-gathering trip to Chambersburg, Pennsylvania.

138. This Stonewall Brigade colonel distinguished himself at Second Manassas by retrieving the fallen colors of the 33rd Virginia and leading a counter attack, his final act.

Southern Women

139. She designed the Stars & Bars or First National flag of the Confederacy.

140. Fannie A. Beers wrote *Memories,* the story of her career serving the South in this capacity.

141. Antonia Ford, caught supplying intelligence to these two cavalry leaders, died as a result of the horrid conditions in the Old Capitol Prison, where she was held.

142. She wrote *Macaria*, which predicted a bleak future if emancipation were to take place. Yankee Gen. George H. Thomas banned the 1863 work.

143. She aided Confederate prisoners at Fort Delaware and Southern wounded in Philadelphia hospitals.

144. After the war, she gave Beauvoir to the state of

Mississippi as a home for Confederate veterans.

145. She wrote *Richmond During the War: Four Years of Personal Observations,* as well as tending the wounded.

146. She administered Robertson Hospital in Richmond and was the only woman commissioned in the C.S.A.

147. Phoebe Yates Pember became a Southern guiding light in this position.

148. She served muddy water at her "starvation parties" in Richmond.

149. This black lady cared for Arlington House during Gen. Lee's war time absence.

150. Her likeness appeared on Confederate currency.

151. Name the granddaughter of former U.S. president John Tyler who raised the First National flag on March 4, 1861, in Montgomery.

152. These Southern belles made the first Battle Flags.

153. She was known as "the daughter of the Confederacy."

154. Who was mocked by Richmond society as the "Empress Eugenia"?

155. She was a Confederate intelligence operative who traveled to Canada to pick up a dispatch for Jefferson Davis.

156. She was the first woman to die in battle.

157. This Confederate spy led raids on Federal outposts in western Virginia. She was captured in July 1862 but shot her guard and escaped on a stolen horse.

158. The $2,000 in gold sewn into her skirt caused this Confederate spy to drown when the ship bringing her back from England went down.

159. What Southern patriot was married to Brig. Gen. John Pegram for just three days before he was killed in action?

160. Who were the Mississippi Nightingales?

161. A Rebel veteran once said that Napoleon would have "laureled" this group of women.

162. Mrs. Jefferson Davis adopted this black boy during the war.

163. Yankee Gen. Benjamin "Spoons" Butler, provoked by the actions of women in this Southern city, issued his infamous General Order No. 28, also known as the "Woman Order".

164. During the Peninsular Campaign this well-known lady of the Confederacy was twice caught behind Federal lines and restored to Confederate territory.

165. This Confederate spy from Martinsburg, Virginia, fled to England when her exploits put her in the Yankee limelight.

166. Brig. Gen. John Hunt Morgan married this spunky patriot just before his Christmas Raid in 1862.

167. She aided 41 Confederates in escaping from the Rock Island, Illinois, P.O.W. camp.

168. This Confederate spy's commendation from Jeb Stuart for her "patriotism, fidelity and ability" earned her a stay in the Old Capitol Prison.

169. During the bombardment of Sabine Pass, this

proprietoress of the Catfish Hotel took hot coffee, doughnuts and meat to Confederate soldiers.

170. Who organized the Mississippi Nightingales?

171. She organized the Wilmington Ladies' Soldiers Aid Society to help the wounded.

172. She was the Angel of Fort Fisher.

Patriots All

173. He was convicted of trying to burn New York City for the South and was hanged.

174. This provisional governor of Kentucky died at Shilo.

175. This South Carolina congressman was known as the Father of Secession.

176. Charleston's leading cotton shipper, John Fraser & Co., was headed up by this Southern patriot and finance expert.

177. Virginian John Bell Yates was hanged by the Yankees for his intelligence-gathering activities and for attempting to capture this ship.

178. The only time this actor wore a real uniform was during John Brown's raid.

179. This author wrote *The Private History of a Campaign that Failed* after serving with the Marion Rangers of Missouri.

180. Two Yankees had to pull on his legs when he was hanged as a spy in Little Rock because he weighed so little.

181. U.S. Congressman Clement Vallandigham, a pro-

Southern Ohioan, was arrested on the orders of this Unionist when he expressed his oppositions to the loss of civil rights.

182. His eyes were gouged out, his tongue was pulled out and he was strangled with a piece of leather because he was a spy for the South.

183. This Southern patriot shot Col. E. Elmer Ellsworth, making him the first Yankee martyr of the War.

184. Massachusetts dandy Sen. Charles Sumner insulted a South Carolina senator and was later caned by this South Carolina congressman, a relative of the offended politician.

185. In what city was Confederate hero Sam Davis hanged as a spy?

186. Name the two Chief Justices of the Supreme Court 1801-1864, both of whom were slave holders and favored state's rights.

187. Poet Sidney Lanier served with this Georgia unit before being captured on a blockade runner and imprisoned at Point Lookout.

188. He furnished photographs of Federal units in Baton Rouge to the Confederates.

189. This Southerner sympathiser, the Supreme Commander of the Sons of Liberty, dreamed of a new Confederacy in the North.

190. He was the most successful of Jeb Stuart's scouts and spies.

191. This Marylander burned Chambersburg, Pennsylvania, at the command of Gen. McCausland when the town refused to pay an indemnity of $100,000 in gold (or

$500,000 in greenbacks).

192. Who was the proprietor of the Marshall House, Alexandria, Virginia?

193. This Prussian fought bravely with J.E.B. Stuart until he was badly wounded.

194. This farmer could say the Civil War began in his back yard and finished in his front room.

195. Jefferson Davis called him "Hill the Faithful."

196. After firing one of the first shots of the war, this septugenarian shot himself in 1865 because he was unwilling to live under the U.S. government.

197. Lt. Col. Arthur Fremantle was on detached duty from this famous foreign unit.

198. He was the only man lost in Stuart's ride around McClellan's Army in 1862.

199. This Catholic priest, chaplain of the 10th Tennessee, lost his life while hearing a confession at Jonesboro, Georgia.

200. Yankee Gen. Benjamin "Spoons" Butler ordered this New Orleans gambler hanged for pulling down a U.S. flag.

201. This family from Christiansburg, Virginia, suffered 18 dead during the War of Southern Independence.

202. When this Wilmington, North Carolina, rector refused to offer prayers for Abraham Lincoln, his church was turned into a hospital.

Notable Quotes

203. According to legend, his last words were "strike the tent."

204. To whom did Nathan Bedford Forrest explain his success by "get there first with the most men?"

205. Who bade farewell to the South by saying, "Wayward sisters, depart in peace"?

206. This Southern commander observed, "The enemy's signals give him a great advantage over me."

207. This Southerner told Lee, "unless he [Grant] offers us honorable terms, come back and let us fight it out."

208. Who said: "Historians are the camp followers of the victorious army?"

209. He insisted that secession was "a necessity and not a choice."

210. While lying mortally wounded at First Manassas, he challenged his fellows with "They've killed me boys, but never give up the field."

211. Who said "We are not fighting for slavery. We are fighting for independence"?

212. Twice the vice-president of the U.S. and Secretary of State for a year, he died in 1850 lamenting, "The South, the poor South."

213. This Northern general said, "There is a class of people in the South who must be exterminated."

214. Who said, "War means fighting, and fighting means killing"?

215. This Confederate surgeon said of Lincoln, "He is one of the greatest scoundrels unhung."

216. Speaking for secession and local rights, he said he would fight "for his side of the street."

217. This Lincoln cabinet member bragged, "If I tap that little bell, I can send you to a place where you will never hear the dogs bark."

218. This Southern hero said of the Yankees: "Those people delight to destroy the weak and those who can make no defense; it just suits them."

219. This Yankee general railed against the Lincoln administration, proclaiming that "the ordinary rights under the Constitution and laws of the country have been violated."

220. At this battle Lee said, "It is well that war is so terrible — we should grow too fond of it."

221. At 1st Manassas, this Southern leader observed, "This army has accumulated a supply of baggage like that of Xerxe's myriads."

222. Who described Nathan Bedford Forrest as "the most remarkable man in our Civil War produced by either side."

223. At Spotsylvania this Southerner declared, "I shall come out of this fight a line major general or a dead brigadier."

224. Who said, "The world has never seen better soldiers than those who followed Lee"?

225. This Lincoln Cabinet member declared, "It was very important that the Rebels strike the first blow in the conflict."

226. Yankee general Charles A. Whittier spoke of what army when he recognized that it "will deservedly rank as the best army which has existed on this continent, suffering privations unknown to its opponent"?

227. This Confederate leader said, "My men don't show to advantage in camp . . . but sir, you should see then when they are fighting — then I would not mind if the whole world were looking on!"

228. This Southern colonel said, "No Confederate who fought at Shiloh has ever said that he found any point on the bloody field easy to assault!"

229. Who described Gen. Braxton Bragg's tactics as "the sparring of the amateur boxer, not the crushing blows of the trained pugilist."

230. This Mississippi congressman said, "The army that

21

invades the South to subjugate her will never return; their bodies will enrich Southern soil."

231. Who issued this proclamation on June 5, 1861: "All rules of civilized warfare are abandoned, and they proclaim by their acts, if not on their banners, that their war-cry is 'Beauty and Booty'"?

232. Who said "No civilized nation within my knowledge has ever carried on a war as the United States government has against us."

233. He said, "My first impulse would be to free all the slaves and send them to Liberia, to their native land."

234. After the War, Lee said "If I had forseen the use those people designed to make use of their victory, there would have been _____."

235. This infantry general said he had "never seen a dead soldier wearing spurs."

236. At Stones River, Gen. Benjamin F. Cheatham shouted "Give 'em hell, boys!" Not wanting to utter a profanity, this general shouted "Give them what Gen. Cheatham says!"

237. Of what officer was this said: ". . . you have quarreled with every officer in the army, and now you are quarreling with yourself."

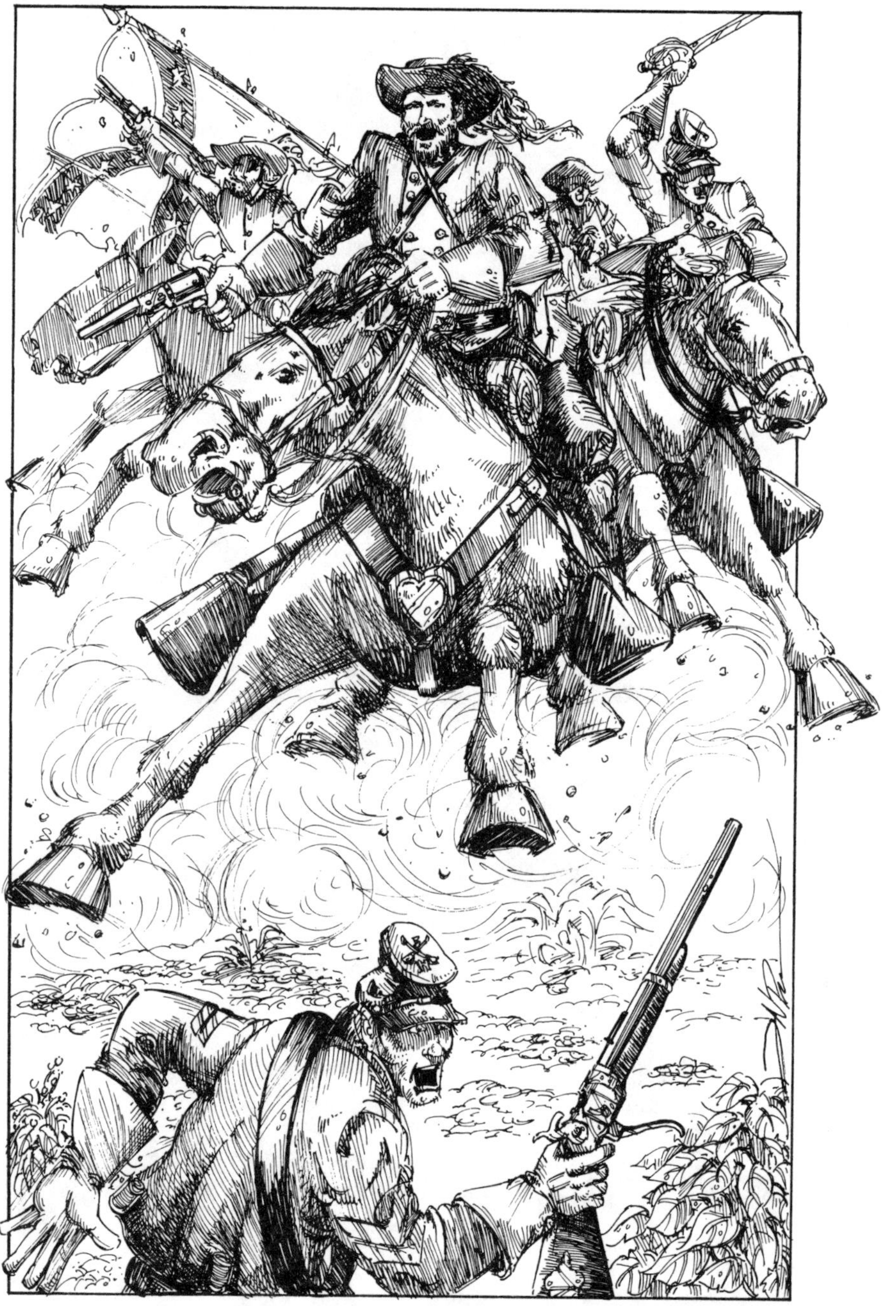

In the Ranks

Units

238. This New Orleans militia unit mustered 4,500 members, mostly foreigners.

239. This Mobile, Alabama, militia unit was comprised of Hispanics.

240. The Washington Artillery was from this city.

241. This drummer boy in the Elliot Grays (6th Virginia) enlisted at age 13 and served from 1861 to 1865.

242. According to South Carolina records, he was the only black to be carried on the state's Confederate roster.

243. Who were the first galvanized Yankees?

244. What is the difference between a dragoon and a cavalry man?

245. By what name was Virginia's First Brigade popularly known?

246. Who commanded the Black Horse Cavalry at First Manassas?

247. What was the official designation of the unit known as Mosby's Rangers?

248. This 19,000-volunteer unit from Georgia was divided into infantry, cavalry and artillery.

249. For what accomplishment is the 7th Tennessee Infantry Regiment, C.S.A., best remembered?

250. Who commanded the Virginia Military Institute cadets at New Market?

251. How many blacks served in the Confederate army?

252. At Murfreesboro, one half of this regiment was armed only with sticks when it attacked the Yankees.

253. How many V.M.I. cadets supported Gen. Breckinridge at New Market?

254. Why did Gen. U.S. Grant disband the 109th Illinois Regiment?

255. Thomas's Highland Legion was comprised of members of what group?

256. When Stonewall Jackson entered Frederick, Maryland, with 40,000 men, how many of his force were black?

257. What North Carolina brigade suffered nearly 50% losses on the first day at Gettysburg?

258. Who commanded the South's Light Division?

259. What number of soldiers constitutes a regimental color guard?

260. What corps of the army was responsible for surveys of defense?

261. The Confederate cavalry used this name for the first sergeant.

262. In what order are the companies of a regiment posted in formation?

263. A gunner on an artillery piece held this rank.

264. Members of this battery had their own choral group known as the Howitzer Glee Club.

265. Most batteries took their name from their captain. This battery took its name from a wealthy Richmond businessman who purchased the guns and all equipage.

266. How many regiments of engineers were there in the Confederate army?

267. This regiment had the greatest percentage of loss on both sides during the war, 82.3% at Sharpsburg.

268. How many Confederate regiments suffered casualty rates of at least 40%?

269. Brig. Gen. Albert Pike's command was a very unusual brigade with three regiments of Indians and Capt. O.G. Welch's squadron of cavalry from this state.

270. How many regiments and how many brigades were involved in Pickett's Charge?

271. Only this arm of the prewar United States army had a majority of Southern officers.

272. Near Macon, Georgia, the militia made up of _____ and _____ charged Union veterans three times on November 22, 1864.

273. At Petersburg on June 9, 1864, 125 old men and boys of this outfit repulsed 1,300 Yankee cavalrymen in three different assaults.

274. The Army of Northern Virginia had how many cavalry

divisions comprised of how many brigades each in 1863?

275. Two companies of Cherokees served with this North Carolina regiment.

276. After creating the Hampton Legion, Gen. Wade Hampton went on to command this unit.

277. What became of the Army of the Allegheny?

278. This army had the longest reprieve from battle of any Confederate army during the war.

Uniforms and Equipment

279. Maj. Gen. John Pope's hat was a prize of this Jeb Stuart raid.

280. This model saddle was used by the artillery on the wheel horse.

281. What was the purpose of a martingale?

282. When was the McClellan saddle introduced?

283. Black trim on a C.S.A. uniform denoted this branch of the service.

284. Script "I" buttons manufactured by P. Tait were made where?

285. This dashing Southern general's uniform was distinctive because of his red battle shirt.

286. This Southern state furnished more uniforms than any other.

287. This hat cover was inspired by those used by British troops in India.

288. Describe a Confederate Marine Corps button.

289. In today's slang, what is a "sardine can?"

290. **AVC** on belt plate or button designated this unit.

291. Why did the boys in Gray commonly carry their bed roll over the left shoulder?

292. All Southern Army personnel were to be supplied with this type of foot gear.

293. Name the famous sword maker of New Orleans.

294. This type of belt buckle was imported from England in great quantities.

295. After the war many Southerners had only their uniforms to wear; they had to cover these items so they would not be wearing "criminal" coats.

296. In the early days of the War for Southern Independence, a Phraigian-style cap was often worn; it was an off-shoot of this Revolutionary War headgear.

297. This Yankee general's captured coat was put on display in Richmond.

298. What is the decorative knot which graces an officer's kepi called?

299. This was the most popular headgear in Southern armies.

300. The presence of an Austrian knot on a uniform indicated what?

301. What was a roundabout?

302. From what was the dye butternut made?

303. A shirt worn as a uniform jacket early in the war was referred to as this.

304. Wearing a Pelican either on accoutrement plates or buttons indicated a soldier was from this state.

305. These two types of belt buckles were designed to save brass and lead.

306. This famous North Carolina regiment had its own belt plate.

307. This state's accoutrement plates used the palmetto tree device and the date 1776.

308. This homemade field pack used by Confederates contained almost everything they owned.

309. Most soldiers had only this in which to cook while in the field.

310. What was Edward Porter Alexander's only signal equipment at First Manassas?

311. Why did the Confederacy manufacture more shell jackets than frock coats?

312. Capt. Samuel Richardson of the 3rd Texas went to war wearing pants made from the skins of this animal.

313. To save leather, many cartridge box slings, rifle slings and belts were made of what material?

314. The South imported thousands of knapsacks from what manufacturer in England?

315. Infantry leather gear imported from England was of this pattern.

316. J.A. King of Mobile, Alabama, manufactured these for

the Confederate Medical Corps.

317. Many of the soldiers carried these poked through two button holes in their jacket.

318. Henry H. Sibley patterned this piece of equipment after the Indian shelters he'd seen while serving in the west before the war.

319. A Signal Corps canteen was made of copper and was large enough to hold a gallon of this type of liquid.

320. Before a large engagement, a soldier might pin a piece of paper on his jacket with this information.

Flags, Symbols and Decorations

321. In the antebellum U.S., what military decoration were there?

322. When was the Southern Cross of Honor first presented?

323. What was the motto of the Confederate army?

324. The Laurel Brigade used this device as a unit insignia.

325. These two Southern states each included a star in its military motif.

326. The addition of an eighth star on the First National Flag signified that this state had joined the Confederacy.

327. He authorized adding the names of battles to Confederate battle flags.

328. This was the popular name of the Third National Flag.

329. Lee's personal flag of a dome of nine stars with a floor of four was based on the design of this flag.

330. The Georgia state flag of the period lacked the postwar inclusion of this symbol.

331. This was the only military medal awarded in the C.S.A.

332. The motto of the Confederate States of America is in Latin *Deo vindice*. What does it mean in English?

333. Which of the Southern flags was never officially adopted by the Confederate Congress?

334. Name the first state to include the battle flag in its state ensign.

335. The raising of the First National Flag over this store in Denver on April 24, 1861, nearly caused a riot.

336. This symbol was the sign of Southerners in Maryland.

337. A Southerner could be arrested in Maryland for wearing these two colors; they indicated support for the Confederacy.

338. How many Davis Guard medals were presented?

339. The Confederate flag salutes these two states that did not secede.

340. The proper name for the national and state flags carried by a regiment.

341. Name the type of flag carried by cavalry units.

342. In a regimental formation, where are the colors posted?

343. How did Gen. P.G.T. Beauregard's design for the battle flag differ from the adopted flag?

344. What banner flew over the first session of the Confederate Congress?

345. How many stars did the final version of the Confederate Stars and Bars have in its union?

346. This state's flag was carried the farthest forward at Gettysburg and Chickamauga.

347. These two dates appear on the North Carolina state flag.

348. What is a "stand of colors"?

In Camp

349. What was a commutation fee?

350. In stabilized areas, Southern pickets traded Yankee pickets tobacco and whiskey for these two items.

351. What was "coosh"?

352. What was sick roll in the Southern army called?

353. During the winter 1863-1864, this was the daily ration for Southern fighting men — when it was available.

354. What was the pay of a Southern private in 1861?

355. What was the Furlough and Bounty Act?

356. In 1861, the Confederacy required this term of enlistment.

357. What was the name of the so-called haunted farm near Charles Town, at Smithfield, Virginia, (now West Virginia) that attracted curious soldiers?

358. What was the amount of the reward paid for the apprehension of deserters?

359. This type of bread was a staple in the Southern army.

360. Sometimes when a soldier was found intoxicated, he had this sign hung around his neck and was paraded around.

361. This term described the punishment practice of tying up a soldier and stuffing something in his mouth.

362. Yankee pickets challenged intruders with "What regiment are you with?" What phrase did Southerners use?

363. The Army of Tennessee called these "nausea."

364. Longstreet's Corps considered these food items a real treat when they served with the Army of Tennessee in 1863.

365. These businessmen traveled with the armies and contracted to sell items to soldiers in the field.

366. Although the penalty for desertion was death, the percentage of actual executions was well under ___% in the Southern Army.

367. Soldiers on leave from Fort Fisher attended this theater in Wilmington, North Carolina.

Combat and Tactics

368. The name given to a fortification of felled trees, their branches facing out.

369. These two men jointly developed the semaphore system in 1859.

370. Who was the Angel of Marye's Heights, and why was he so named?

371. When a soldier said he had "seen the elephant" what did he mean?

372. In battle, this tactic produced the heaviest losses for the South.

373. Confederate forces rolled these down on the advancing enemy from Missionary Ridge.

374. How much fighting took place when Virginia troops captured the U.S. arsenal at Harpers Ferry?

375. At First Manassas, how was Brig. Gen. N.G. Evans warned that his flank was about to be turned?

376. This man-made obstacle at Marye's Heights helped the Confederate Army.

377. Name the place designated for bringing together military supplies for distribution.

378. Soldiers built these from earth and heavy timbers to protect themselves from artillery shelling.

379. What man-made geographic feature did Toombs's Georgians make use of at Sharpsburg?

380. Which Confederate general wrote the *Infantry Drill Manual?*

381. When marching down a road, how many columns wide was the march?

382. In the Peninsular Campaign, Confederate Gen. John Magruder's troops were shelled by Yankee Capt. John Tidball's battery of regular artillery. What did these two men have in common?

383. How many ranks were in a battle line?

384. These men used flags to send coded messages.

385. Gen. Jubal Early blamed nearly all his failures in the Valley Campaign of 1864 on this branch of the service.

386. Gen. Jubal Early ordered these personal items to be left behind in order to ensure a quiet march in his predawn attack at Cedar Creek.

387. He was Lee's confidential telegrapher and tapped Grant's lines for about six weeks in 1864.

388. Name the telegrapher who sent disinformation to the Yankees about Gen. Morgan's raids.

389. The Confederate infantry preferred to use this march step.

390. Gen. John Magruder promoted Pvt. Sharpe of the 1st North Carolina Infantry to corporal for this personal favor.

391. As Lee began to withdraw his Southern forces at Gettysburg, this took place at Vicksburg.

392. Why was the death of Union abolitionist Maj. Theodore

37

Winthrop at Big Bethel ironic?

393. What field condition slowed the charge of the Virginia Military Institute cadets on May 15, 1864?

394. Morgan's exceptionally skilled telegrapher carried this nickname.

395. In telegraphic code, the Federals knew him as "Andes".

396. After a battle started, band members were usually assigned to what duty?

397. The most compact defensive Confederate battle line (16,000 men per mile) was used here.

398. This was the greatest concentrated Confederate frontal assault — 15,000 men in a half mile front.

399. What is the military term for attacking the enemy as an enemy attack is failing?

400. This was sometimes called so the wounded on both sides might receive help.

401. A skirmisher who could shoot straight was sometimes called this.

402. What was the "fog of war?"

403. The name given a log laid on the top of a trench to help give cover and from which to shoot under.

404. The term given to sharpened sticks shoved in the ground pointing toward the enemy to slow his advance.

405. Predawn attacks were very successful when masked by this natural phenomenon.

406. This was the most common form of military

communications.

407. Henry Kyd Douglas once rode how many miles in 20 hours as a courier for Stonewall Jackson?

408. Col. John S. Mosby's wagon train raid near Berryville, Virginia, (August 1864) was jeopardized when a Confederate gun was placed over this unseen hazard.

409. The first Confederate kill of the War was Yankee Thornberry Brown, killed in action near this Virginia (now West Virginia) town.

Weapons

410. The foundation of the Southern armament industry was this Northern enterprise.

411. The Confederate observation balloon was made of this material.

412. This dentist-turned-inventor developed a new ignition system for firearms.

413. This two-barrelled handgun was developed by a French-born New Orleans physician and manufactured in France.

414. The Harpers Ferry armament factory was moved to what Southern city?

415. This former U.S. master armorer became the superintendent of all Confederate armories.

416. This Southern arsenal produced most of the arms for the Cause manufactured domestically.

417. Which firm manufactured the 1842 Palmetto musket?

418. Give the proper name of the Austrian rifled musket used in the War.

419. In what town was the Georgia Armory located?

420. Bilharz, Hall & Co. carbines were manufactured where?

421. The action of this carbine or rifle could be fired independently of the barrel and stock.

422. The S.C. Robinson Co. of Richmond produced a Southern version of this carbine.

423. Brig Gen. Turner Ashby favored this edged weapon.

424. This Richmond firm produced edged weapons for the Cause.

425. What calibre was buck and ball?

426. What was the most common rifle calibre used 1861-1865?

427. What was the purpose of the artillery short sword?

428. What was a Fougass?

429. What was pommeling?

430. About one-half of the C.S.A.-manufactured artillery tubes were made by this company.

431. Name this English-made, breech-loading 12-pound artillery piece.

432. Which was longer, the Enfield rifled musket or the Enfield rifle?

433. For what specialized use was the .45 calibre Whitworth rifle employed?

434. The double-action .36 calibre Adams was a favored sidearm of Southern soldiers. Where were they made?

435. The state of Virginia imported nearly 1,000 of these English-made, spurless, .44 calibre double-actions before the war.

436. These Texas brothers produced pistols for the Cause.

437. Most Confederate-made handguns were copies of this Northern-produced weapon.

438. What inducements were given to weapons manufacturers in the South?

439. How many pistols did the South produce during the conflict?

440. Upon examination of Southern gun emplacements after First Manassas, Gen. McClellan was embarassed to find these.

441. Where were Leech and Rigdon pistols manufactured?

442. Confederate-made pistols by Spiller and Burr were close imitations of this Northern-made weapon.

443. This pistol had UNITED STATES SOUTH stamped on it.

444. In June 1862, this was established as the official calibre for all Confederate longarms.

445. More than 50 Hughes 1-1/2 or 2" breechloaders are thought to have been made by this Memphis firm in 1862-1863.

446. The accuracy and distance of this weapon made frontal assaults on fortified positions suicidal.

447. Leech and Rigdon, producers of pistols, made swords

41

under this company name.

448. What percentage of long arms did the South import?

449. Only one of this type of once-common cannon was employed by either side at Gettysburg.

450. What was the largest cannon that the Army of Northern Virginia took on campaign?

451. This newly invented anti-personnel device was first used at Yorktown by Confederate forces.

452. This company manufactured the largest number of pistols for the Confederacy.

453. By the manual, how many steps does it take to load a rifled musket?

454. This imported rifle used interchangeable ammunition and bayonets and would stack with the Springfield-pattern weapon.

455. What was the most commonly used artillery piece on either side?

456. This punch-type, powder-train zinc time fuze was designed for artillery shells and case shot.

457. This shoulder weapon was preferred by Gen. Nathan B. Forrest's cavalry.

458. What is the military term for artillery firing on enemy artillery?

459. What is military term for artillery firing on enemy infantry?

460. What two wheeled vehicle is often confused with a caisson?

461. How many percussion caps were issued in a pack of ammunition?

462. The city of Charleston rejoiced when this Yankee gun blew up.

463. Through his efforts, it could be said the armies never lost a battle due to a shortage of gun powder.

464. Many churches donated their bronze bells to supply these for the Confederacy.

465. His innovation in artillery shells was to form a segmented polyhedral cavity that would burst into a

predetermined number of pieces.

466. In Fort Pulaski, the Confederates removed one of these from its mountings and employed it as a mortar.

467. Many of the imported French 12 pounders were made by this company.

468. He telegraphed the state of South Carolina January 17, 1861, "Will make anything you want - work night and day if necessary, and ship by rail."

469. Some Confederates thought they could fight with only these for weapons in 1862, but they were never used in combat.

470. What calibre pistol did the Navy adopt?

471. What was carried in a pass box?

472. How was the purchase price of cannon barrels determined?

473. What was manufactured at the Tyler Ordnance Works in Tyler, Texas?

474. This rifle bore the Stars and Bars on the lock plate.

475. This Confederate carbine was manufactured at Greenville Military Works and was one of the most advanced, firing a .50-calibre center-fire cartridge.

476. Several thousand of these revolvers were run through the blockade from England.

477. Maj. Gen. Patrick Cleburne's sword was engraved with a shamrock on the hilt and this on the scabbard.

478. What did Leech & Rigdon, McElroy & Company and the Nashville Plow Works all produce?

479. Many Confederates carried these for camp use and personal defense.

480. Cartridge boxes for rifled muskets were designed to carry how many rounds of ammunition?

481. A single package of ammunition contained how many individually wrapped cartridges?

482. This English import cavalry saber was often carried by Confederate troops.

483. The 30-pounder Parrot gun captured by the Confederates at First Manassas was given this nickname.

484. What was the most favored and important of the cavalry weapons?

485. Which carbine was favored above all others North or South?

486. Which Southern-manufactured pistol appeared to be "slab sided" because of no recoil shield?

487. The term "gun" properly refers to this type of weapon, not a rifled musket.

488. He was the owner of Bellona Arsenal foundry in Chesterfield, Virginia.

489. He invented a smooth bore breechloading cannon that fired buckshot.

490. The Claiborne Machine Works of Nashville manufactured these in six, twelve and thirty-two pound sizes.

491. Who invented the double barrel cannon?

492. Tappey and Lumsden invented this type of cannon.

45

493. The Georgia pike had an 18-inch blade mounted in this manner.

494. How many new model 1855 rifled muskets were captured at Harpers Ferry in 1861?

495. The Richmond Armory manufactured the two band Navy musketoon in this calibre.

496. Between July 1, 1861, and January 1, 1865, the Richmond Arsenal manufactured how many muskets?

Forts, Prisons and Hospitals

497. In July 1862, 36 Confederate prisoners escaped from this Illinois penitentiary on the Mississippi River through a tunnel.

498. The Hygeia Hotel was built on the same land as this Virginia fort which remained in Northern hands.

499. Name the northernmost of the two forts on Sullivan's Island near Charleston.

500. The Charleston Zouave Cadets manned this fortification.

501. Where was Castle Thunder?

502. This ship chandlers warehouse in Richmond was better known as what prison?

503. What was the official name for the Andersonville Prison?

504. This Confederate general was responsible for all prisoners held in Southern P.O.W. camps east of the Mississippi River.

505. What was the original use of the Old Capitol Prison in Washington, D.C.?

506. Confederate prisoners of war were held at this camp between the Potomac River and Chesapeake Bay.

507. The North held about how many Southrons as political prisoners?

508. This key witness against Capt. Heinrich H. Wirz of Andersonville Prison admitted perjury after the former commandant had been hanged.

509. What was the largest Confederate P.O.W. camp run by the North?

510. Name the Confederate hospital complex in Richmond, Virginia.

511. How many Yankees were killed during the shelling of Fort Sumter?

512. Where was Fort Negley?

513. Southern doctors were held as P.O.W.s by this Yankee general after Shiloh.

514. The Tishomingo Hotel in this town became a medical-surgical center after the Battle of Pittsburgh Landing.

515. At the start of the hostilities, how many medical doctors were there in the Confederate army?

516. Confederate doctors did not remove these pests from wounds because they removed dead tissue, which helped to prevent gangrene.

517. He was villified in the North as being responsible for the deaths of tens of thousands of Yankee P.O.Ws.

518. Where in Virginia was the Ladies Relief Hospital?

519. At age 19, he was the South's youngest commissioned

medical officer.

520. This Quaker doctor served Confederate wounded in Lynchburg, Virginia; he reduced the mortality rate from 75% to 5% when smallpox hit.

521. This former U.S. Senator-turned-Confederate-colonel rowed out to Fort Sumter to ask Maj. Robert Anderson to surrender.

522. Name the two Confederate earthen forts at Port Royal, South Carolina.

523. This fort helped to protect Charleston harbor; it dates from the Revolutionary War.

524. This brick fort guarded the entrance to Mobile Bay.

525. This was the strongest fortress of the Confederacy. It held until January 15, 1865.

526. This fortress was used by the Federals as headquarters for the "On to Richmond" drives.

527. These two Charleston-area forts were seized the same day (December 27, 1860).

528. Did more prisoners die in the P.O.W. camps of the North or the South?

529. Fort Sumter had placements for 140 guns, but only this many were ready for use April 12, 1861.

530. How many shells were fired at Fort Sumter by the South Carolinians?

531. The Yankees identified the bastioned earthwork at Knoxville as Fort Sanders; the Confederates referred to it by this name.

532. He commanded Fort Fisher when it capitulated following the Northern naval shelling.

533. Maj. Heinrich Wirz was commandant of what prison?

534. He was director of Chimborazo Hospital.

535. Castle Pinckney was occupied on December 27, 1860, by these Southern troops.

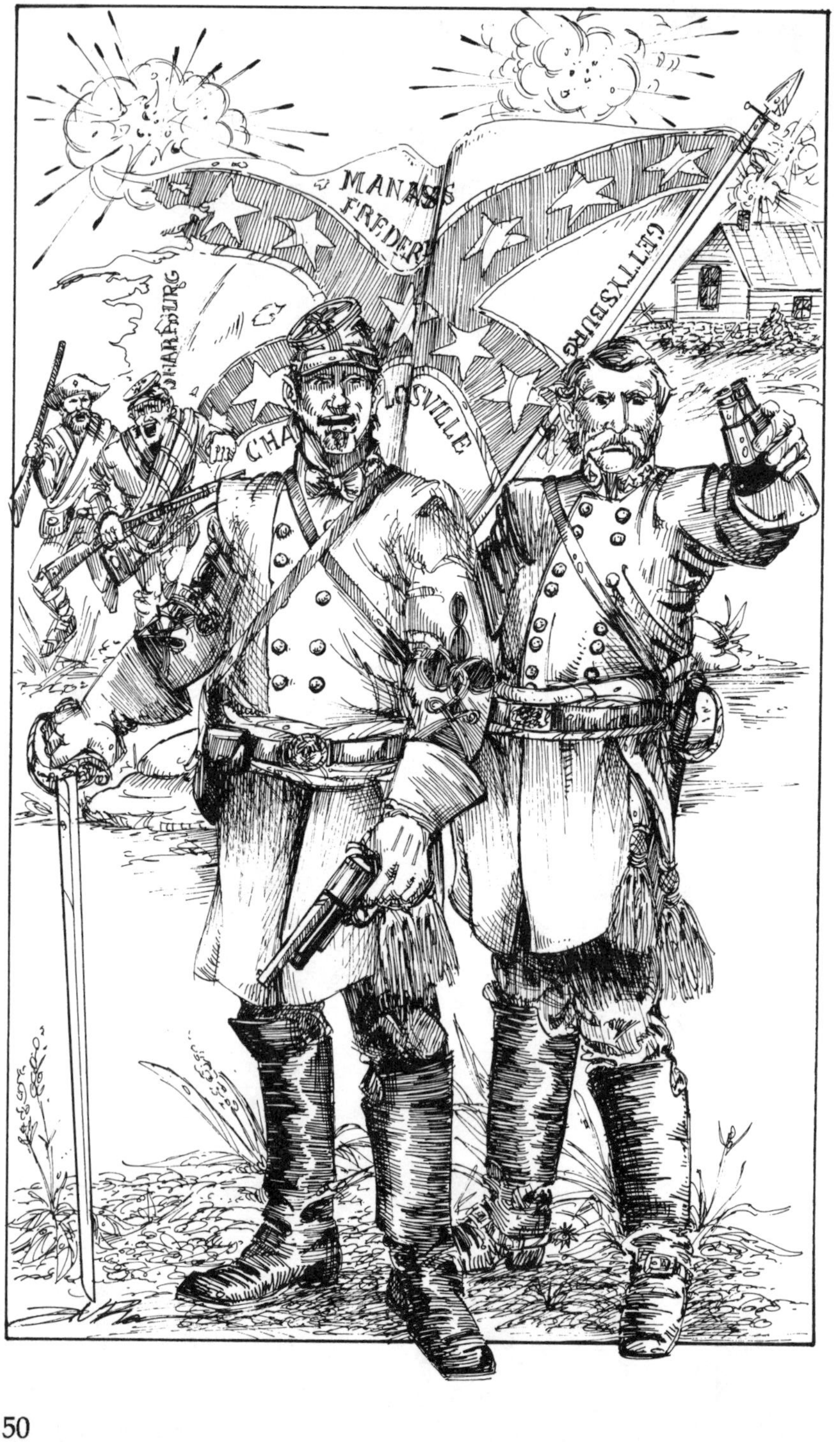

MANASS
FREDER
GETTYSBURG
CHA

Total War

War in the East

536. What percentage of Lee's Army was captured at Sayler's Creek?

537. The Battle of Cedar Creek deprived Lee of this vital commodity.

538. The Battle of Brandy Station pitted these two cavalry leaders against each other.

539. Who led the raid on Coggin's Point, Virginia, September 14, 1864 (later called the Cattle Raid)?

540. What Confederate victory led the Union to create The Committee on the Conduct of the War?

541. What was the Confederate name for the Battle of Pea Ridge, Arkansas?

542. What were the dimensions of the Atlanta Campaign from Chattanooga, Tennessee, to Jonesboro, Georgia?

543. Vicksburg was under siege for how long?

544. He was the only Southern officer to pierce the Northern line during Pickett's Charge.

545. What was the time spread between First and Second Manassas?

546. Before the battle, a Confederate column moved on Gettysburg in search of what item?

547. The first land battle of the War was fought here on June 10, 1861.

548. What percent of Southern soldiers were killed or wounded at Gettysburg?

549. How many Confederate soldiers and civilians were trapped at Vicksburg?

550. His Yankee troops pillaged the Shenandoah Valley and burned the Virginia Military Institute.

551. Lee and 60,000 men repulsed Grant's attempt to take Richmond with 117,000 men in this battle.

552. The Rebel yell was first heard at this battle.

553. What was Gen. George Pickett's troop strength the day of the "high water mark of the Confederacy"?

554. Why were Southern forces forced to evacuate Petersburg, Virginia?

555. It took Gen. S.D. Sturgis 9 days to march 7,800 Yanks from Memphis to Brice's Cross Roads to attack 3,500 patriots in gray, but only this long to scoot back to Memphis in defeat.

556. In this battle of June 27, 1862, Lee had the numerical advantage and drove the Yankees from their defensive positions.

557. Why was the Battle of Gaines's Mill a very costly victory for the South?

558. This battle broke the spirit of McClellan's Peninsula army but at a fearful loss to the South; nearly 25% of Lee's army were casualties.

559. What was the Southern objective of Second Manassas?

560. Who commanded the Southern forces at the sunken road in Sharpsburg, Maryland?

561. Two Georgia regiments commanded by Brigadier General Robert Toombs held up the Yankee army on Antietam Creek at this crossing.

562. Every brigade commander was killed in this furious assault.

563. How many days did the beseiged Southerners hold on before Petersburg was finally lost?

564. What Yankee general urged his troops to leave the South as "chimneys without houses"?

565. Blacks in blue first fought Confederate blacks in this battle.

566. This officer of the 33rd Virginia Infantry (whose militia uniforms were blue) had his men dress ranks and fix bayonets; in this manner they boldly captured Northern artillery pieces at First Manassas.

567. Stonewall Jackson's command caught Maj. Gen. O.O. Howard's XI Corps having dinner at this church during the battle of Chancellorsville.

568. Three days prior to this battle, Gen. J.E.B. Stuart's cavalry held a massive review on the very ground where blood would flow; and, amazingly, he repeated the review two days later for Lee.

569. At Gettysburg, the first attack unexpectedly came from this direction when a Confederate brigade ran into Brig. Gen. John Buford's cavalry.

570. Florida was saved for the Confederacy in this battle.

571. Who commanded Lee's right wing at Gettysburg?

572. Whose Mississippians opposed the laying of pontoon bridges at Fredericksburg?

573. Stonewall Jackson broke this corps, which triggered the Yankee stampede at Chancellorsville.

574. His Southern division assaulted the McPherson Farm at Gettysburg.

575. Pvt. B.W. Mitchell of the 27th Indiana found three cigars wrapped in this important document.

576. This cavalry brigade covered Lee's retreat from Gettysburg.

577. What was the name of the mill at Chickamauga?

578. This bridge was held by Southern Gen. Toombs's Brigade at Sharpsburg.

579. The name given to an unusual bulge in the Confederate line at Spotsylvania.

580. This was the last major land battle of the war.

581. The only cannon lost by Lee when crossing the Potomac after Sharpsburg had been captured at First Manassas from what Federal battery?

582. This Southern commander was captured with nearly his entire corps at Sayler's Creek.

583. In February 1865 Lee's position here was seriously threatened; engineer troops fought in their own trenches to repel the Federals.

584. The Federals ignored what telltale signs that might have warned them of Stonewall Jackson's imminent attack upon the XI Corps at Chancellorsville?

585. This house at Cedar Mountain was prophetically named.

586. Earthworks here were dug in 1781, but deepened by "Prince John" Magruder in 1862.

587. This little log church gave its name to one of the bloodiest battles of 1862.

588. In this engagement the 1st Maryland (C.S.A.) fought the 1st Maryland (U.S.A.) in hand-to-hand combat, brother fighting brother.

589. In September and October of 1864 Sheridan burned the Shenandoah Valley, precipitating this battle.

590. This might have been called the Silent Battle. Confederate troops at Cold Harbor could see but not hear this battle unfold.

591. This battle took place on the island of the Lost Colony.

592. The first Federal general captured was seized as he slept on a pile of mailbags on a train stopped in Harpers Ferry.

593. Who owned the peach orchard at Gettysburg?

594. What were the losses suffered by the Army of Northern Virginia at Gettysburg?

595. At the Battle of Gettysburg, the Southern army almost ran out of this essential item.

596. Prior to the Battle of Groveton, Virginia, this Southern commander ordered his lieutenants to "bring up your men, gentlemen."

597. During the retreat from Gettysburg, the citizens of this Pennsylvania town cut the wheels of wagons carrying Confederate wounded.

598. Prior to this major battle, bands from each side played for the boys.

599. The 26th North Carolina suffered 71% casualties in this battle.

600. When did the infamous pillaging of the South by the Yankee Sherman commence?

601. This was the final confrontation in the Seven Days' Battles.

602. The Battle of Murfreesboro was given this name by the Southerners.

603. Two Union repeating guns, forerunners of the Gatling Gun, were captured during this part of the Peninsular Campaign in 1862.

604. Who were Pickett's three brigade commanders at Gettysburg?

605. During what battle (May 25, 1864) did Gen. Joseph E. Johnston repulse Union attacks near Pumpkin Vine Creek?

606. This battle was actually three separate engagements at Turner's Gap, Fox's Gap and Crampton's Gap.

607. For what length of time was Fort Sumter bombarded by South Carolina troops?

608. Yankee Benjamin "Spoons" Butler's attempt to stun Fort Fisher on December 23, 1864, failed when this exploded.

War in the West

609. Col. Santos Benavides and his cavalry regiment kept open the trade routes with Mexico to assure a supply of this important commodity for the Confederacy.

610. Cuban-born Joseph A. Quintero served in Virginia and later was transferred to the Confederate diplomatic service as an agent in this country.

611. His "Buffalo Hunt" claimed New Mexico for the Confederacy.

612. This Indian tribe was considered to be the most steadfast to the Southern Cause.

613. Control of this pass was the key to securing eastern Tennessee.

614. The Confederate highwater mark in the Rocky Mountain West occurred when Henry Hopkins Sibley occupied this capital city.

615. He was called the Stonewall Jackson of the West.

616. Confederate Lancers from Texas were deployed in this battle.

617. How many Confederates accepted the surrender of the New Mexican garrison at Cubero with its 49 men, 60 muskets and 2,000 rounds of ammunition without a shot being fired?

618. This stove designer commanded Southern troops in Confederate New Mexico.

619. Why was Maj. Gen. Braxton Bragg not with his army at the battle of Perryville?

620. This Russian-born Yankee "closed his eyes" so his men could burn Athens, Alabama.

621. In which battle did the Round Forest (known to both sides as "Hell's Half Acre") figure?

622. "Strike for your altars and your homes" was a motto of this Texas outfit.

623. In Wild West style, his brother Bill and a few cavalry scouts took prisoners after riding their horses through the Gayoso House hotel in Memphis.

624. The 3rd Colorado Volunteer Cavalry (U.S.A.) under the command of Col. John Chivington massacred 500-600 Cheyennes led by this chief.

625. How large was the Territory of New Mexico in 1861?

626. A convention in Tucson elected him a delegate to the Confederate Congress.

627. The Confederacy established the Territory of Arizona with this present-day New Mexican town as the capital.

628. He was the self-appointed governor of the Confederate Territory of Arizona.

629. Name the first pitched battle between Unionists and Confederate forces in the intermountain west.

630. Some Texas troops were armed with this type of pole arm in New Mexico.

631. This U.S. general surrendered all Federal property under

his control in Texas to the Confederacy and was appointed a major general C.S.A.

632. President Davis proclaimed this battle "The Thermopylae of the Civil War."

633. Name the only battle in which the Confederate Government issued medals to the soldiers.

634. He commanded the Army of the Mississippi at the battle of Perryville.

635. Not one of the Virginia Lees, he fought at Chickasaw Bluffs.

636. This Confederate commander opposed Yankee Gen. Nathaniel Banks in the Red River Campaign.

637. The Overton home was his headquarters at Nashville in 1864.

638. He rode with William Quantrill and his killing earned him the nickname "Bloody" in the North.

639. This Kentucky-born cavalryman was active in almost every campaign west of the Mississippi.

640. What was the name of the mess hall built by Hood's Texans in the winter camp of 1861-62?

641. In the winter 1861, Gen. Albert Pike and Col. Douglas H. Cooper organized these five Indian nations into three regiments.

642. This battle pitted Confederate Indians against Union Indians in a draw that left over 500 dead.

643. Gen. John Bell Hood replaced him as commander of the Army of Tennessee.

644. How many Confederate generals fell at the Battle of Franklin?

645. This Stevenson, Alabama, hotel was used several times as a military headquarters.

646. On January 1, 1863, Gen. John Magruder attacked this port city and won it after four hours of combat.

647. He commanded the Confederate Indians who were accused of scalping dead Yankees after the battle of Pea Ridge, Arkansas.

War at Sea

648. How many Union vessels did the Confederacy capture with the fall of the Norfolk Navy Yard?

649. As commander of the C.S.S. *Florida,* he destroyed or captured 34 vessels.

650. Where was the C.S.S. *Alabama* built?

651. The blockade-runner *Fingal* was refitted as this ironclad.

652. Received too late to be commissioned the C.S.S. *Stonewall,* she instead sailed under this flag.

653. The crew of this Confederate ram included three free blacks.

654. This famous gun sank the U.S. gunboat *Cincinnati.*

655. A few miles off the Galveston, Texas, coast, the C.S.S. *Alabama* sank this Union ship.

656. This Confederate Chief of Naval Ordnance began design work on the first C.S.A. ironclads.

657. The fear that Southern ironclad ships would break the blockade caused what "disease" in the North?

658. One of the last to surrender at Sayler's Creek, this C.S.N. captain later became an admiral in the Peruvian Navy.

659. He commanded the Confederate submarine *David* when it attacked the Yankee vessel *New Ironsides.*

660. He began his service for the Confederacy by heading up the Confederate Lighthouse Service.

661. As governor of South Carolina, he permitted the firing on

the *Star of the West* which was to provision Fort Sumter.

662. He and Chief Engineer William Williamson began turning the scuttled U.S.S. *Merrimack* into an ironclad.

663. What was the mission of the U.S.S. *Commodore Jones* when she was destroyed by a Confederate electric torpedo?

664. The U.S.S. *Housatonic* was destroyed by this Confederate privateer submarine.

665. Name the first Southern ironclad to do battle with the invaders.

666. He headed up the Confederate Marine Corps at its inception.

667. By 1864, what were the chances of running the Yankee blockade successfully?

668. What percent of U.S. naval officers resigned their commissions to serve the Confederacy?

669. This Annapolis graduate organized the Confederate Naval Academy.

670. The C.S.S. *Patrick Henry* served this specialized use.

671. He commanded the C.S.S. *Tallahassee* and took more than 30 prizes off the New England coast.

672. This Southern ship survived the War but sank off Yokohama in 1869.

673. In April 1863 this "unsinkable" monitor sank in Charleston Harbor after being struck with more than 90 rounds.

674. The southern coastline was divided into how many

blockading zones by the North?

675. The first Northern naval base in the South was in this city.

676. Gen. McClellan postponed his combined operations plan because of the presence of this Confederate ship.

677. This Confederate ram was used successfully to support the relief of Plymouth, North Carolina, in 1864.

678. This ram ran through the Union fleet at Vicksburg.

679. This Union vessel was first fired on by South Carolina artillery on on January 9, 1861.

680. She was the first ship to proudly raise the Confederate flag.

681. On February 17, 1864, this Confederate vessel was the first submarine to sink a ship.

682. While teaching at Annapolis, he wrote "Elements of Seamanship" and other naval manuals.

683. He was in charge of Southern conscription until December 1862, when he was made chief of the Torpedo Service.

684. Name the Charleston Harbor steam tug that was renamed the *Lady Davis* in honor of the First Lady of the Confederacy.

685. Most of the blockade runners leaving this island colony were bound for New Orleans or Mobile.

686. This Confederate vessel was captured on the James River on July 4, 1862, when she ran aground.

687. Most of the blockade runners bound for ports on the

Atlantic coast used one of these islands as a jumping off place.

688. He built electronically detonated torpedoes for the Confederacy.

689. He captured and sank over 20 enemy ships during his service on the C.S.S. *Clarence*.

690. The C.S.S. ram *Tennessee* and C.S.S. gun boats *Selma*, *Morgan* and *Gaines* were built in this city.

691. She was the last C.S.A ship to sail the open sea.

692. The surrender of this revenue cutter was the first Federal ship taken by a Southern state.

693. What was the minimum age for acceptance in the Confederate Naval Acadamy?

694. How did the South first use iron armor?

695. Jefferson Davis authorized privateers with the issuance of these documents.

696. Why did naval guns of the period use round shot?

697. This ship was the first recognized Southern privateer.

698. Jefferson Davis promised to do this if Confederate privateers were hanged as pirates.

699. This was Capt. Raphael Semmes's first command.

700. The C.S.S. *Alabama* was identified by her builders as No. 290, but was also called by this name.

701. Why did Arthur Fremantle go on a chicken-killing spree on the C.S.S. *Fingal*?

702. Why did blockade runners use anthracite coal?

703. Why did blockade runners vent their steam under water?

704. Why was the first Southern attack on the *Star of the West* ignored by official Washington?

705. Confederate commissioners James Mason and John Slidell were illegally removed from the British steamer *Trent* by Capt. Charles Wilkes, who commanded this Union vessel.

706. What was the immediate reaction of the British to the *Trent* Affair?

707. How many ships did the C.S.S. *Alabama* capture on her 21-month voyage?

708. The Confederate Navy Works was located here.

709. What was the name of the Confederate submarine designed to operate as an underwater ram?

710. What was the largest number of vessels in the Confederate Navy at one time?

711. The *Alabama* captured how many ships on her reign of the seas?

712. Over a period of 13 months, the C.S.S. *Shenandoah* sank how many ships and captured how many prisoners?

713. This ship was known as "The Emperor of China's Yacht."

714. Blockade runners were usually painted this color.

715. These two ironclads were built in Wilmington, North Carolina.

War on Rails

716. The Andrews Raid involved these two railroads.

717. Northern troops on the Bermuda Hundred threatened this railroad.

718. Confederates derailed a Federal train at this Virginia station and smashed another into the wreckage.

719. Maj. Gen. Braxton Bragg maneuvered his troops southward from Mobile to Atlanta and then to Chattanooga in the first use of this.

720. This railroad was the major link between Southern forces

in the Western theater and the East Coast.

721. At the outset of the War the North had 22,000 miles of railroad tracks. How many did the South have?

722. This Federal locomotive was nearly captured on the Orange and Alexandria Railroad near Union Mills on August 1, 1863.

723. This railroad line went through the town of Harpers Ferry, Virginia.

724. When the War began, how many railroads were there in the South?

725. This Confederate captain chased the "General" in the engine "Texas" until he got her back.

726. The United States Military Railroad was comprised primarily of what?

727. Eastbound B & O trains carried grain for the Yankee army and this for its navy.

728. Stonewall Jackson hoodwinked this president of the B & O and captured many of his trains.

729. After seizing 56 locomotives and 386 railway cars, Stonewall Jackson burned another 67 locomotives in this city.

730. In railroad terminology, what were "U-rails"?

731. This railroad tragedy happened September 13, 1863, near Asworth, Georgia, when a train carrying this precious cargo was hit by another train.

732. How many railroad cars were required to move an 1863 regiment of infantry?

733. Longstreet's Corps traveled how many miles by rail to support Gen. Bragg in 1863?

734. This railway connected Gordonsville and Richmond.

Strategy

735. What did the Confederacy hope to accomplish at of the Battle of Pilot Knob?

736. This Southern action prompted the North to muster 75,000 troops.

737. Lee divided Jackson's corps between these two military leaders.

738. How did the tactics of Gen. John Hunt Morgan differ from other Confederate cavalry leaders?

739. Stonewall Jackson faced how many Union armies in the Shenandoah Valley in the spring of 1862?

740. In the spring 1862, Stonewall Jackson won five of six battles with the invaders; but more importantly he kept this many Federals away from Richmond.

741. Lincoln suspended the writ of *habeus corpus* to combat Southern sympathizers on what date?

742. After their defeat at Second Manassas, the Union army fled northeast, to this city, leaving supplies scattered behind.

743. Lee divided his army into how many small corps (including J.E.B. Stuart's cavalry) prior to the battle at Sharpsburg, Maryland?

744. When Lee's army invaded Maryland, another Southern army commanded by this general invaded what other

Union-controlled state?

745. Southwestern Virginia mines supplied these two essential minerals to the Confederacy.

746. Gen. John Bell Hood's invasion of Tennessee was designed distract this Yankee in the East.

747. What was Pres. Buchanan's goal in January 1861?

748. Within 90 days of Fort Sumter's capitulation, President Davis was criticized for turning down 200,000 enlistees. Why did he?

749. Generals P.G.T. Beauregard and Joseph E. Johnston did not heed this officer's advice to rush the aggressor's army after the victory of First Manassas.

750. He established the "Long Kentucky Line" from the Mississippi River to the Virginia line.

751. With the Northerners firmly in control of Port Royal, he made a strategic decision not to defend the coast lines.

752. When Lee took command, he divided the Army of Northern Virginia into how many corps?

753. Afraid to face Confederate infantry at Manassas after the stunning Southern victory of 1861, Yankee general McClellan devised this plan to employ naval power.

754. When Lee moved his army west to Chancellorsville, to whom did he entrust the security of Fredericksburg?

755. Although outnumbered nearly two to one, Lee split his army in May 1863 and sent Stonewall Jackson around the enemy's right flank in this battle.

756. This suggestive title was the name of the 1861 Federal plan to strangle the South.

757. Once this network was complete, the Southern economy nearly came to a halt.

758. How much indemnity did the Confederates demand of Frederick, Maryland?

759. Having promised to fight it out "if it takes all summer," Grant abandoned his position at Spotsylvania and moved to protect this spot.

760. Rather than face capitulation at Appomattox, this Southern officer suggested to Lee that "we would scatter like rabbits and partridges in the woods, and they could not scatter to catch us."

761. Grant was delayed in his Vicksburg Campaign when Confederate Gen. Earl Van Dorn destroyed $1 million worth of Yankee supplies here.

762. This Virginia community was ordered burned by Gen. John Magruder when events dictated its fall to the invaders.

763. This Gen. J.E.B. Stuart lieutenant bluffed Custer's Yankee cavalry into believing Charlottesville was protected by a large Southern force.

764. According to an old soldier's adage, the amateur warrior studies tactics, but the professional warrior studies this.

765. By ignoring these two bridges, Gen. Braxton Bragg allowed the Yankees to cross the Chickamauga uncontested.

766. By holding this mountain, Bragg kept the Army of the Cumberland bottled up in Chattanooga for a month on half rations.

Geography

767. Big Shanty, Georgia, is now known by this name.

768. Antietam Battlefield is in this county.

769. The Battle of Glorieta Pass was fought in this canyon.

770. The war was nearly over when Grant reached this southern river.

771. This inland city was the home of the C.S.A. Naval Yard after Norfolk and Portsmouth were destroyed.

772. The court house cupola in this county was used as an observation platform during the Battle of Vicksburg.

773. What is the northern boundary of the Shenandoah Valley?

774. The Peninsula of Virginia is bounded by these two rivers.

775. On October 19, 1864, Gen. Jubal Early lost a large portion of his artillery supplies and wagons of wounded because of a broken bridge in this town.

776. Franklin's Crossing on this river figured in the Fredericksburg Campaign.

777. The largest city in the South during the Civil War.

778. The Battle of Fort Donelson was fought near this creek.

779. This Virginia (now West Virginia) town was the first to be torched by Yankees.

780. The Pensinsula of Virginia is dissected by this river.

781. McClellan headed for the Yankee fleet on this body of water in his retreat from Gaines's Mill.

782. Where did the Southern army cross the Potomac on Lee's first invasion of the North?

783. Buildings in this town were destroyed by Yankee general "Spoons" Butler in anticipation of an attack that never happened.

784. When Port Hudson, Louisiana, fell, the captors found many barrels of this precious commodity.

785. Jackson's men earned the nickname of "Foot Cavalry" during a lightning march through this valley.

786. Arlington House and the Lee-Custis estate were used by Yankee forces for what purpose?

787. This creek figured in the Battle of Brice's Cross Roads.

788. This Alabama city was the industrial center for the deep South.

789. Confederate defenses of this Southern city were 90 miles away, at Plaquemine Bend.

790. The Third Battle of Winchester was fought on this stream.

791. Lee ordered Gen. J.E.B. Stuart halt his independent raids and rejoin the Southern army when Union Gen. Joseph Hooker crossed this river.

792. This city was the key to controlling the Mississippi River.

793. Morgan's last major raid ran through which two Northern states?

794. The Bermuda Hundred is a crooked neck of land between these two rivers.

795. What river figured in the Battle of Cedar Creek?

796. This creek figured in the Battle of Perryville.

797. This natural barrier runs from Georgia through Harpers Ferry.

798. Where is Ziegler's Grove?

799. Confederate sharpshooters at Devil's Den fired at the enemy across this creek.

800. This creek figured in the Battle of Sharpsburg.

801. This stream figured in the Battle of Manassas.

802. Lee deployed his troops on the banks of the swollen Potomac River near this western Maryland town.

803. In the language of the Cherokees, the name of the Chickamauga River means this.

804. What was the 2nd largest city in the South in 1860?

805. In what mountain range are the Manassas, Ashby's, Snicker's and Chester gaps?

806. This stream figured in the Battle of Gettysburg.

807. This town name means "place of peace" in Hebrew.

808. This river figured in the Battle of Franklin.

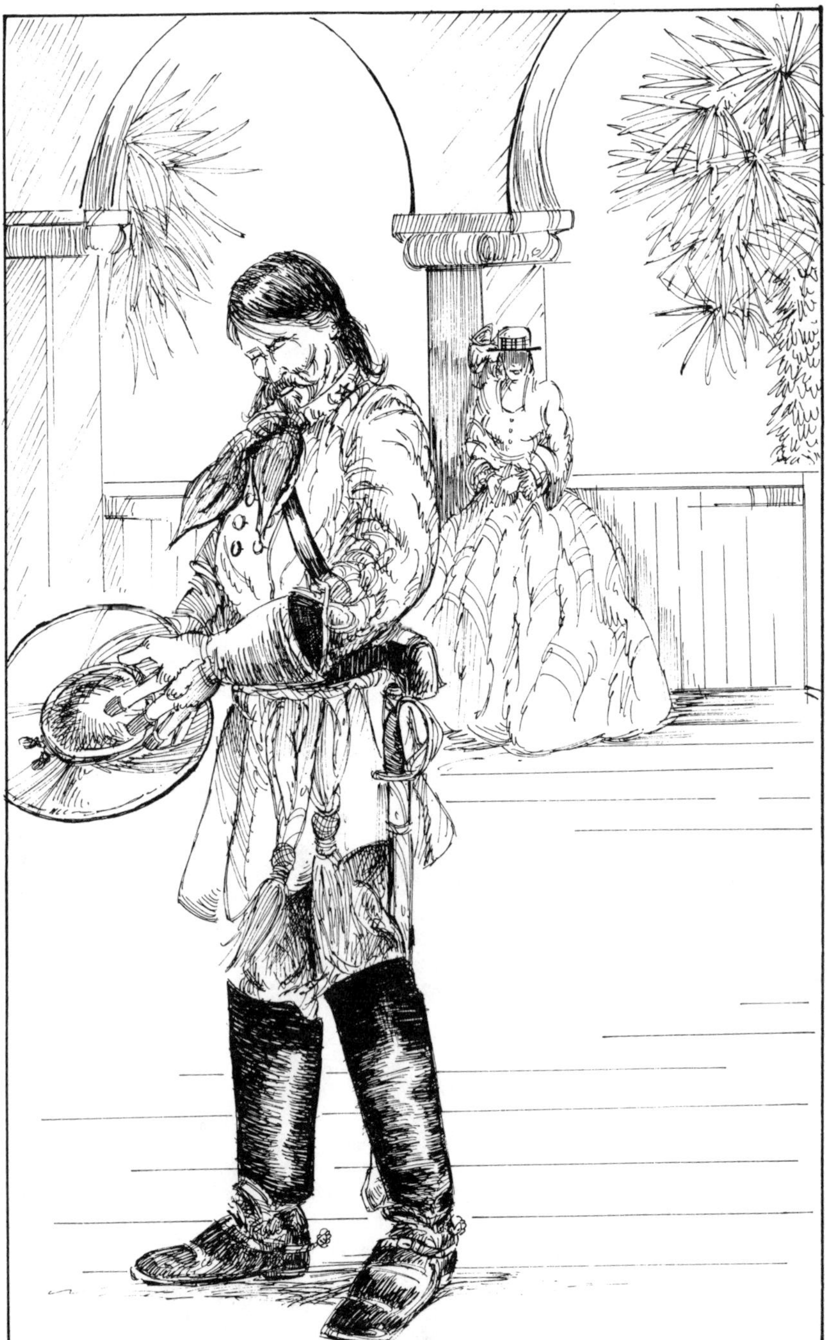

The Cause

Politics and Government

809. Prewar plantation aristocrats primarily belonged to this political party.

810. Martin Crawford, Alfred Roman and John Forsyth formed an embassy to Washington, D.C., to plead for this action.

811. This black man was the official greeter at the White House of the Confederacy.

812. What was the size of the Confederate Government's debt at the end of the war?

813. What post did John Reagan hold in the C.S.A. government in 1862?

814. Born in Connecticut and hanged in Virginia, this fanatical abolitionist coldly murdered innocents in Kansas.

815. How many members were in the Confederate House of Representatives?

816. How many Confederate Senators were there?

817. This colonel of the 17th Alabama served as attorney general for the Confederacy until elected governor of Alabama.

818. Who was the treasurer of the provisional Confederate government?

819. Because of inflation, the Confederate government authorized this amount of new currency to be printed in February 1864.

820. Who was the chief of the Confederate Navy?

821. Who was Chief of Exchange of Prisoners for the Confederate Government?

822. He was in charge of the C.S.A. Medical Department.

823. When was a provisional constitution for the Confederate States of America adopted?

824. What role did Southern gentlemen Yancey, Mann and Rost play in supporting the South?

825. He was appointed by the Confederate Government to organize the Southern Telegraph Co. as a private company.

826. What did the Confederate Roll of Honor supplant?

827. When did the Confederate capital move from Montgomery to Richmond?

828. He was the last Confederate Secretary of the Treasury.

829. Where did the last Confederate cabinet meeting take place?

830. When was the Congress of the Confederacy dissolved?

831. He and the Virginia delegates lobbied the central government to move from Montgomery to Richmond.

832. By June 1, 1861, the Confederate Government had taken

over or established how many post offices in the South?

833. In 1862 the war was so unpopular in the North that this general wrote to Secretary of War Edwin Stanton, "We have now more treason in the army than we can well get along with."

834. The postal clerks' strike in Richmond was broken by the institution of this process.

835. When did the concept of a southern nation first come about?

836. The military use of stampless mail was called what?

837. When Lee posted a letter, he placed this on it instead of a stamp.

838. Mail service between the North and the South ceased on this date.

839. What term describes an alliance or league for mutual support or action?

840. He represented the Confederate War Department in England.

841. This C.S.A. cabinet officer entered Yale at age 14, graduated at 17.

842. This vice president of the C.S.A., a Georgia attorney and former U.S. congressman, had the best understanding of constitutional issues in the South.

843. In January 1848, in the U.S. House, he said, "Any people anywhere . . . having the power, have the right to rise up and shake off the existing government and form a new one that suits them better."

844. Name the Atlanta mayor who surrendered his city to the Union army.

845. Whose South Carolina homes were special targets for Sherman's fire starters?

846. This Washington hotel was the gathering spot for both Northern and Southern statesmen in antebellum days.

847. This former U.S. president served in the Confederate Congress.

848. He served in the Confederate Cabinet as Attorney General, Secretary of War and Secretary of State.

849. Who was the C.S.A. Secretary of the Treasury in 1862?

850. He expelled all Jews from the Department of Tennessee with threat of imprisonment if they returned.

851. The antebellum mayor of this large Northern city proposed his city become an independent republic to avoid conflict.

852. This Kentucky senator's family was split by loyalties North and South. One son became a general for the Cause and the other achieved the same rank in the Northern forces.

853. War appeared inevitable February 4, 1861, when peace commissioners failed to reach accords in this city.

854. This former Southern governor served as a courier between President Davis and General Lee.

855. This U.S. president asked Congress to pass the "Force Bill", which would allow him to use the army and navy against any state not enforcing the 1828 and 1832 tariff laws.

856. He resigned his U.S. Cabinet post when Pres. James Buchanan refused to order U.S. troops out of Fort Sumter.

857. This French Ambassador was the only foreign emissary to visit both the North and the South during the war.

858. He was governor of North Carolina and colonel of the 26th North Carolina Infantry.

859. This state lent the C.S.A. government $500,000.

860. Union Gen. Nathaniel Banks prevented this state's legislature from meeting by arresting Southern-oriented members, thus preventing a quorum.

861. This political party was designed to thwart the expansion of slavery.

862. What percent of Southern troops were from North Carolina?

863. Mayor T.J. Goodwyn surrendered this city when assured by Sherman that it would be safe; it was, however, sacked and burned.

864. The Lincoln administration arrested two Congressional candidates in this border state in 1863.

865. More than 30 blacks were killed in this Northern city's anti-draft riots July 13-16, 1863.

866. This Illinois governor virtually dissolved his state's general assembly for two years to staunch pro-Southern and anti-war feelings.

867. Name the governor of Colorado who authorized the arrest of Southern sympathizers.

868. How many Southern sympathizers were tried by U.S. court martial after Lincoln suspended civil liberties?

869. This Maryland governor attempted to negotiate peace between North and South with Lord Lyons of Great Britain acting as mediator.

870. It took 30,000 troops under Union Gen. John Dix to keep the peace in August 1863 in this northern city.

871. James G. Berdet, the pro-Southern mayor of this city, was required to resign his elected office as a condition of his release from the Union prison at Fort Delaware.

872. Not only was it illegal for blacks to enter this Northern state, any person who employed a black could be punished.

873. The spectators at this antebellum event included Lee, Jackson, Jefferson Davis and J.W. Booth.

874. Despite the Lincoln folklore of today, this Northern state forbade blacks to move there.

875. Name the Southern agent in England who represented C.S.A. Naval Secretary Stephen Mallory.

876. The North applauded this secession while rejecting Southern Separatism.

877. Lincoln's first choice as a running mate in 1864 was despised in the South for his repressive measures.

878. This high-ranking U.S. military man thought the South should be allowed to secede in peace.

879. When conscription began in the South, this governor took the central government to court to contest its legality.

880. This was the first of the pro-Southern border states upon which Lincoln inflicted martial law.

881. Who was the wartime governor of Virginia?

882. This state had the fewest members in the Confederate House of Representatives (2).

883. This state held the most seats in the Confederate House of Representatives (16).

884. This Texas governor, born in Virginia, opposed secession and the War of Rebellion.

885. These three were the only states to ratify secession ordinances by popular vote.

886. How did President Lincoln inadvertently give legitimacy

to the Southern Cause?

887. In the antebellum period, Albert Sidney Johnston held this sensitive cabinet post in the Republic of Texas.

888. He was the Mayor of Richmond during the war.

889. When Maj. Anderson fled from Fort Moultrie to Fort Sumter, this South Carolina governor sent a messenger to protest.

The Homefront

890. The citizens of Winchester, Virginia, saw their town change hands how many times during the War?

891. Between 1861 and 1864, what was the rate of inflation in the South?

892. These two Yankees freed slaves in their geographic command areas before the Emancipation Proclamation was issued.

893. Water, yeast and ginger root, with molasses for color and flavor, were the ingredients in this popular drink of the time.

894. European reliance on this Southern agricultural product was a forlorn hope.

895. How many slaves were freed by the Emancipation Proclamation?

896. Built in 1637 and equipped in New England as a slaver, she was the first Anglo-American ship to import slaves to Massachusetts.

897. This state legislated to end to slave importation in 1778.

898. He gave the majority opinion in the Supreme Court's Dred Scott Decision but manumitted his own slaves.

899. Cotton was not the economic king of the South in 1860; this commodity was economically more significant.

900. He founded the Knights of the Golden Circle.

901. This Yankee general made sure Arlington House would never be used as a residence again by burying Union dead as close to the Lee home as possible.

902. What was the population of the South in the 1860s?

85

903. The largest immigrant group in antebellum Richmond was from this country.

904. What was the first colony in America to codify chattel slavery?

905. When was slavery abolished in Washington, D.C.?

906. What was the population of the North in 1861?

907. In what year did the U.S. Congress outlaw the importation of slaves?

908. The last known illegal slaver foundered off the coast of this state in 1858.

909. Name the most successful slave traders in the U.S. in 1860.

910. This was the only place in the U.S. where former owners were compensated for slaves freed by law.

911. The Sons of Liberty, the Knights of the Golden Circle, the Corps de Belgique and the Order of American Knights were seen as reprehensible in the North and legally labeled what?

912. According to U.S. Census Bureau records, how many free blacks were there in the slave states in 1860?

913. About 50% of all Southerners were one of these three nationalities.

914. How many free blacks were there in Virginia in 1861?

915. How many free blacks were there in the South in 1861?

916. What was the price of a barrel of flour in January of 1864? (A soldier's pay at that time was $18 per month.)

917. What would two dollars or a pair of socks get you in Uniontown, Alabama?

918. For the first time, this holiday was not observed in the South in 1861.

919. How much of Atlanta was destroyed by fire?

920. What was the name given to the dried balls of coal dust and sawdust mixed with clay and sand that were used to heat Southern homes?

921. Blacks represented what percent of the population in the antebellum South?

922. What was the name of U.S. Grant's slave of antebellum days?

923. A family's groceries in Richmond in 1860 averaged $6.65 weekly; in 1863 this inflation had driven the price up to this amount.

924. Free blacks and slaves worshiped here in wartime Richmond.

925. Wilmington, North Carolina, was wracked by this disease in 1862.

926. What percent of Southerners owned slaves?

Music, Words and Images

927. "Dixie" was first formally used in the South on this occasion.

928. In the Southern army, these two musicians were assigned to infantry companies.

929. This Confederate general claimed "Cheer, Boys, Cheer"

87

as his campaign or marching song.

930. As Lee's army marched into Maryland during the first invasion of the North, his soldiers sang this song.

931. Between July 1861, and February 1862, this Richmond firm delivered 111 drums to the Confederacy.

932. It was in this Southern city, shortly before his death, that Lincoln asked his military band to play "Dixie".

933. Who composed "When Johnny Comes Marching Home"?

934. This action, triggered when a Federal brigade band struck up a lively march, nearly destroyed a bridge on the Rappahannock at Fredericksburg.

935. This black pianist traveled and performed throughout the South.

936. What was the most widely published Rebel song of the War?

937. "God Save the South" was written by George H. Miles but published under this pseudonym.

938. What was the favorite marching song of Hood's Texans?

939. How many songs were written and published in the Confederacy during the War?

940. Daniel D. Emmet wrote the words and music to this popular song in 1860.

941. This former-Zouave-turned-combat-artist sketched the Shenandoah Valley.

942. This large news-gathering organization had more reporters covering the war than any individual

newspaper.

943. Name Mathew Brady's two top assistants.

944. This paper image was the photographic rage during the war.

945. This Corinth, Mississippi, photographic firm recorded Federally occupied Vicksburg.

946. From inside Fort Sumter, this Southerner photographed exploding Yankee ordnance striking the fort.

947. Reporter and artist Edwin Forbes worked for what publication?

948. Where were the first C.S.A. notes printed?

949. Who was the author of *The Rise and Fall of the Confederate Government?*

950. These Southern photographers shot stereo views of Fort Sumter three days after Maj. Anderson surrendered.

951. Who wrote the *Southern History of the War?*

952. This man's Federal order caused about 300 newspapers and publications to be shut down.

953. This Philadelphian printed 1, 564, 050 counterfeit C.S.A. notes, but later claimed they were just souvenirs.

954. The date found on the Great Seal of the Confederacy is associated with what other famous event?

955. Felix Kirk Zollicoffer was the antebellum editor of this newspaper.

956. This English officer wrote *Three Months in the Southern*

89

States: April - June 1863.

957. This Confederate general's picture is on the $500 Confederate bill.

958. This Yankee editor called the U.S. Constitution "an agreement with hell" and burned a copy July 4, 1862.

959. President Lincoln bowed to public pressure when a crowd of 20,000 demonstrated against the military control of this newspaper in Illinois.

960. George William Curtis, the editor of this influential publication, compared Lee with Benedict Arnold.

961. This *Richmond Examiner* editor harshly opposed President Davis.

962. This Northern newspaper actively espoused the Southern Cause.

963. The *Gazette* of Franklin County, New York, was banned by the Lincoln administration from using this method of distribution.

964. He was Stonewall Jackson's first biographer.

965. This Yankee brigadier's likeness graced the chamber pots of New Orleans brothels.

966. What was the "City Intelligenzer?"

967. He urged support of the government and army in his 1864 pamphlet entitled "Address to the People of the Confederate States."

968. This poet penned "The Burial of Latané", "Ashby", "Music in Camp" and "Lee to the Rear."

969. Who was the editor of the Charleston *Mercury* from 1860-1862?

970. Telegraphers used a piece of equipment called a pocket telegraph to do what?

971. The first Confederate-issued adhesive postage stamp featured his image on the five-cent stamp.

972. This pro-southern newspaper was published in England to influence British public opinion.

After Appomattox

973. Legend tells us that Lee met Grant under this kind of tree at Appomattox.

974. At Appomattox, this Union general ordered his men to honor the "Boys in Gray" with a final military salute as Southern flags were furled.

975. He was the only officer on Lee's staff to accompany the commander to the Appomattox surrender site.

976. Southern military units were disallowed for this time period during Reconstruction.

977. Captured Southern battle flags were returned during this president's administration, 40 years after the war.

978. This convicted co-conspirator in President Lincoln's assassination was pardoned by President Andrew Jackson in 1869.

979. Convicted of conspiracy in Lincoln's assassination, she was the first woman hanged legally in the U.S.

980. In which year did the United Confederate Veterans form?

981. During the Battle of San Juan Hill in the Spanish-American War, this former Confederate general is reported to have yelled "Look at the damn Yankees run!" as Spanish troops broke.

982. Jefferson Davis's birthday (June 3) is celebrated across the South as what holiday?

983. How long after Lee surrendered was Abraham Lincoln killed?

984. He headed up the anti-Southern clique in the U.S. House of Representatives during reconstruction.

985. The Civil Rights Act of 1866 made all but this group of people eligible for citizenship.

986. The House of Representatives moved to impeach President Johnson after he fired this cabinet member.

987. In 1866, the U.S. Supreme Court found that President Lincoln had illegally done away with civil courts in this case.

988. The Wade-Davis Bill was a precursor of this.

989. This Southern general died March 21, 1891, from a cold contracted while acting as honorary pallbearer for Northern general William T. Sherman.

990. Where did President Davis take possession of what remained of the C.S.A. national treasury?

991. He photographed the execution of Andersonville's commandant, Heinrich Wirz.

992. His hatred of all things Southern spurred on the Black Republicans of the U.S. Senate during Reconstruction.

993. After the war, former general James Longstreet led black

troops in New Orleans against this group.

994. A Mississippi captain who had been wounded in the jaw at Chickamauga found these when visiting the battlefield 32 years later.

995. Who took the photograph of Lee on Traveller after the War?

996. In what year was the Sons of Confederate Veterans founded?

997. This Texas Ranger was the last commander in the South to exercise control in combat.

93

998. This Cherokee was the last Confederate general to surrender.

999. The last surviving Confederate brigadier, he died April 20, 1928, in Waco, Texas.

1000. On what date did the last Confederate veteran, Walter Washington Williams, die?

1001. He commanded the last Confederate troops in the last engagement in the War of the Rebellion.

Answers

SOUTHERN HEROES

Jefferson Davis

1. 1868
2. $100,000 in gold
3. Buena Vista
4. Benjamin F. Butler
5. Vicksburg
6. Joe
7. Rewrite it
8. Estell Hall
9. 1978, retroactive to 1868
10. Twice
11. Metairie Cemetery, Louisiana
12. Finis
13. Thomas Jefferson
14. Spotswood Hotel
15. Major Anderson's withdrawal from Fort Moultrie to Fort Sumter

Robert E. Lee

16. Fort Mason, Texas
17. Greenbrier and Jeff Davis
18. Ulysses S. Grant
19. Not enough men in uniform
20. June 23, 1862
21. Chancellorsville
22. Palm Sunday (April 9, 1865)
23. Blair House, Washington, D.C.
24. Ulysses S. Grant
25. George B. McClellan
26. His farewell to the Army of Northern Virginia
27. April 22, 1861
28. Lucy Long
29. Traveller

ANSWERS

30. Resign

Stonewall Jackson

31. A civilian suit and blue military overcoat
32. John Brown
33. "Tom Fool" or "Old Blue Light"
34. Judah P. Benjamin
35. Harpers Ferry, (West) Virginia
36. Daniel Harvey Hill
37. Guiney's Station, Virginia
38. Jeff Shields
39. Robert E. Lee, then president of Washington College
40. A gum raincoat
41. Hunter McGuire, M.D.
42. Cedar Mountain

Officers and Gentlemen

43. Lewis Addison Armistead
44. Brig. Gen. Turner Ashby
45. John C. Breckinridge
46. Maj. Gen. "Black" David Hunter
47. Patrick Ronayne Cleburne
48. John C. Breckinridge
49. Brig. Gen. John R. Chambliss
50. Leonidas Polk
51. Gen. James Longstreet
52. Joseph Reid Anderson
53. Nathan Bedford Forrest
54. Maj. Jedediah Hotchkiss
55. Gen. Gabriel James Rains
56. Capt. John W. Morton
57. John C. Pemberton
58. John Pegram
59. Lucius Waller (killed) and John Marmaduke
60. James Longstreet
61. Camille Armand Jules Marie de Polignac
62. Lt. Gen. William J. Hardee
63. John Singleton Mosby
64. Fitzhugh Lee and Joe Wheeler
65. Brig. Gen. George E. Pickett
66. Both were Masons
67. John Brown Gordon
68. Brig. Gen. William Barks-

ANSWERS

dale

69. Frank Crawford Armstrong
70. Maj. Robert H. Anderson, U.S.A.
71. Brig. Gen. William E. Baldwin
72. Both were Masons
73. Col. John S. Mosby
74. Fr. John B. Bannon
75. Gen. States Rights Gist
76. Brig. Gen. Reuben L. Walker
77. Maj. Gen. William H.T. Walker
78. Surrender
79. 77
80. Shot while leading frontal assaults
81. 1,000
82. Six
83. Gen. James Longstreet
84. Gen. Nathan Bedford Forrest
85. John Hunt Morgan
86. Shiloh
87. John C. Breckinridge
88. "Prince John" Magruder
89. Joseph E. Johnston
90. 313 (about 1/3 of the officer corps)
91. Gen. John Hunt Morgan
92. Gen. Braxton Bragg
93. Nashville Military Institute
94. Col. Meriwether Thompson
95. Gen. P.G.T. Beauregard
96. Brig. Gen. Thomas B. Smith
97. Daniel Harvey Hill
98. Robert S. Garnett
99. James Longstreet
100. Seven Pines
101. Richard Stoddert Ewell
102. Thomas Jefferson
103. Gen. James J. Pettigrew
104. Gen. A.P. Hill
105. Stones River, Tennessee
106. His father's sword
107. Gen. Turner Ashby
108. Brig. Gen. William N. Pendleton
109. Stephen Dill Lee

ANSWERS

110. Maj. Gen. Jeremy F. Gilmer
111. Champion's Hill
112. Gen. J.E.B. Stuart
113. Capt. John McClanahan
114. Brig. Gen. Joseph "Fightin' Joe" Wheeler
115. Gen. Charles S. Winder
116. Gen. Lewis Armistead
117. Gen. Braxton Bragg
118. A 12-pound cannon
119. William S.H. Baylor
120. 427
121. 146
122. 11%
123. John S. Mosby
124. Quartermaster Gen. Montgomery C. Meigs
125. Old Crow
126. Gen. P.G.T. Beauregard
127. Gen. Felix H. Robertson
128. Lieutenant general — 17 were so commissioned
129. Earl Van Dorn
130. U.S. President Zachary Taylor
131. Windsor, New York
132. Philadelphia, Pennsylvania
133. Capt. James K. Boswell
134. Raphael Semmes
135. Gen. W.H.C. Whiting
136. E. Porter Alexander
137. Turner Ashby
138. William Smith Hanger Baylor

Southern Women

139. Nicola Marschall
140. As a hospital nurse
141. Stuart and Mosby
142. Augusta Jane Evans
143. Margaret Anna Parker Knobeloch
144. Varina Howell Davis (Mrs. Jefferson Davis)
145. Sallie Ann Brock
146. Capt. Sally L. Tompkins
147. Superintendent of Chimborazo Hospital
148. Constance Cary
149. Selina Gray
150. Lucy Holcomb Rickens

ANSWERS

151. Letitia Tyler
152. Constance, Hetty and Jennie Cary
153. Winnie Davis
154. Mrs. Jefferson Davis
155. Lottie Moon
156. Judith Henry of Henry House, First Manassas
157. Nancy Hart
158. Rose O'Neal Greenhow
159. Hetty Cary of Richmond
160. Paid, uniformed women nurses
161. Confederate mothers
162. Jim Limber
163. New Orleans, Louisiana
164. Mrs. Robert E. Lee
165. Belle Boyd
166. Martha Ready
167. Kate E. Perry-Mosher
168. Antonia J. Ford
169. Kate Dorman
170. Sally Reneau
171. Mary Ann Buie
172. Daisy Chaffee Lamb

Patriots All

173. Robert Cobb Kennedy
174. George W. Johnson
175. Robert B. Rhett
176. George A. Trenholm
177. U.S.S. *Michigan*
178. John Wilkes Booth
179. Mark Twain
180. David Dodd
181. Gen. Ambrose Burnside
182. D.S. Jobe
183. James T. Jackson
184. Rep. Preston Brooks
185. Pulaski, Tennessee
186. John Marshall (Virginia) Roger B. Taney (Maryland)
187. Macon County Volunteers
188. A.D. Lytle
189. Congressman C. L. Vallandigham (D-Ohio)
190. Vespasian Chancellor
191. Col. Harry Gilmore
192. James T. Jackson
193. Heros von Borcke

ANSWERS

194. Wilmer McLean
195. Benjamin Harvey Hill
196. Edmund Ruffin
197. The Coldstream Guards, H.M.S.
198. Capt. William Latané
199. Fr. J. Emerson Blimeal
200. William Mumford
201. The Christian Family
202. Dr. A.A. Watson (St. James church)

Notable Quotes

203. Robert E. Lee
204. Gen. John Hunt Morgan
205. Horace Greeley
206. Stonewall Jackson
207. James Longstreet
208. Thomas Carlisle
209. Jefferson Davis
210. Capt. Francis S. Barton
211. Jefferson Davis
212. John C. Calhoun
213. Gen. W.T. Sherman, U.S.A.
214. Nathan Bedford Forrest
215. George Todd, Lincoln's brother-in-law
216. Phillip Lightfoot Lee
217. Secretary of War Edwin M. Stanton
218. Robert E. Lee
219. Gen. John C. Frémont
220. Fredericksburg
221. Gen. Joseph E. Johnston
222. William Tecumseh Sherman
223. Brig. Gen. Abner Perrin, who was killed at the Bloody Angle
224. Theodore Roosevelt
225. Secy. of the Navy Gideon Wells
226. The Army of Northern Virginia
227. Robert E. Lee
228. William P. Johnson
229. Gen. Daniel H. Hill
230. William Barksdale
231. Gen. P.G.T. Beauregard
232. Robert E. Lee
233. Abraham Lincoln
234. "no surrender at Appomat-

ANSWERS

tox Court House."

235. Daniel H. Hill

236. Gen. Leonidas Polk

237. Gen. Braxton Bragg

IN THE RANKS
Units

238. The European Brigade

239. The Spanish Guards

240. New Orleans, Louisiana

241. Charles F. Mosby

242. Henry Brown of the Darlington Guards

243. Former Yankee prisoners of war who joined the Cause

244. A dragoon fights dismounted; a cavalry man while mounted

245. The Stonewall Brigade

246. J.E.B. Stuart

247. 43rd Battalion of Partisan Rangers

248. Phillip's Georgia Legion

249. Capturing the 7th Tennessee, U.S.A.

250. Lt. Col. Scott Shipp

251. An estimated 93,000

252. 44th Mississippi

253. 247

254. Its officers were accused of being Copperheads

255. The Cherokee Nation

256. More than 3,000

257. Alfred Iverson's Brigade

258. Gen. Ambrose P. Hill

259. Eight

260. Corps of Engineers

261. Orderly sergeant

262. From left to right: 1st, 6th, 4th, 9th, 3rd, 8th, 5th, 10th, 7th and 2nd

263. Corporal

264. Richmond Howitzers

265. Purcell

266. Two regiments of ten companies each

267. 1st Texas

268. 50

269. Texas

270. Eleven brigades and 42 regiments

271. The cavalry

101

ANSWERS

272. Old men and boys
273. The Petersburg Home Guard
274. Four cavalry divisions, each with six brigades
275. 69th North Carolina
276. Stuarts Cavalry Corps
277. It was merged with the Army of Northern Virginia
278. The Army of Tennessee (January to June 1863)

Uniforms and Equipment

279. Catletts Station, Virginia
280. The Grimsley
281. Stop the horse from throwing its head
282. 1859
283. Medical Department
284. Limerick, Ireland
285. A.P. Hill
286. North Carolina
287. The havelock
288. A block **M** on a plain field
289. A C.S.A. belt plate
290. Alabama Volunteer Corps
291. To keep the right hand free to use a weapon
292. Jefferson boots
293. Hyde & Goodrich
294. Snake buckle
295. Military buttons
296. The Liberty cap
297. Gen. John Pope
298. A quatrefoil
299. The slouch hat
300. Rank (on the sleeve)
301. A short waisted, single-breasted coat with a low standing collar
302. Oil of the white walnut or cooperas
303. A battle shirt
304. Louisiana
305. Frame type and fork and tongue
306. 6th Infantry
307. South Carolina
308. Bed roll
309. Tin cup
310. One lantern
311. To save material
312. Jaguar

ANSWERS

313. Cotton webbing
314. S. Isaacs, Cambell & Co.
315. Enfield
316. Brass tourniquets
317. Toothbrush
318. Tent
319. Turpentine or other flamables
320. Name and unit for identification

Flags, Symbols and Decorations

321. None
322. July 1900
323. *Aide toi, et dieu t'aidera* (Help yourself, and God will help you.)
324. A sprig of laurel on a heart
325. Texas & Mississippi
326. Virginia
327. Lt. Gen. William Hardee
328. The Stainless Banner
329. First National Flag
330. The Battle Flag
331. Davis Guard medal
332. God will judge
333. The Battle Flag
334. Mississippi
335. Wallingford & Murphy
336. The Bottany Cross
337. Red and white
338. 45-47
339. Kentucky and Missouri
340. The colors
341. Guidons
342. On the left of the right center company
343. The field was blue, the bars red
344. The Bonnie Blue
345. Thirteen
346. North Carolina
347. May 20, 1775 and May 20, 1861
348. A single color or flag

In Camp

349. Payment to keep out of the draft
350. Coffee and newspapers
351. Flour and water fried in grease
352. Company Q

103

ANSWERS

353. One pint of cornmeal and a quarter pound of bacon

354. $11 per month

355. 12-month volunteers would be given a 60 day leave plus $50 to reenlist

356. One year

357. Wizard Clipp

358. $30

359. Hard tack

360. "Drunk"

361. Bucked and gagged

362. "Who is your commander?"

363. Bacon and sweet potatoes

364. Sweet potatoes

365. Sutlers

366. One

367. Thalian Hall

Combat and Tactics

368. Abatis

369. Edward P. Alexander and Albert J. Myer

370. Conf. Richard Kirkland gave water to wounded Federals

371. He had seen battle

372. Frontal assaults on fortifications

373. Boulders and set artillery shells

374. There was none

375. Semaphore flags

376. A stone wall

377. A depot

378. Bomb proofs

379. A stone quarry

380. William J. Hardee

381. Four

382. Both were natives of Winchester, Virginia

383. Two

384. Signalmen

385. Cavalry

386. Canteens and tin cups

387. C.A. Gaston

388. George A. Ellsworth

389. Route step

390. A drink of liquor from his canteen

391. Capitulation

392. He was shot by a black

ANSWERS

member of the Wythe Rifles

393. Wet ground
394. Captain Lighting
395. President Lincoln
396. Attending the wounded
397. Fredericksburg
398. Pickett's Charge
399. Counter attack
400. A truce
401. Sniper or sharpshooter
402. Black powder gun smoke
403. Head log
404. Palisade
405. Fog
406. Courier
407. 105
408. A nest of hornets
409. Grafton

Weapons

410. The captured Federal arsenal at Harpers Ferry
411. Bolts of dress silk
412. Edward Maynard
413. The LeMat revolver
414. Fayetteville, North Carolina
415. James H. Burton
416. The Richmond Armory and Arsenal
417. William Glaze & Co., Columbia, South Carolina
418. Lorenz
419. Milledgeville, Georgia
420. Pittsylvania Court House, Virginia
421. The Hall
422. Sharps
423. 1840 Dragoon Saber
424. Boyle & Gamble
425. .69
426. .58
427. To disembowel horses over-running the guns
428. A land mine
429. In a saber duel, hitting the opponent with the pommel or basket of the saber.
430. Tredegar Iron Works, Richmond
431. Whitworth

105

ANSWERS

432. The musket was 8" longer than the rifle
433. Used by snipers
434. Chicopee Falls, Massachusetts
435. Adams & Deane
436. J.H. Dance and Bros.
437. 1851 Navy Colt, .36 calibre
438. Deferment; loans and guarantees; and loan forgiven if plants captured
439. Less than 10,000
440. Quaker guns (painted logs)
441. Columbus, Mississippi, then Greensboro, Georgia
442. The Whitney
443. Tranter
444. .577
445. Street, Hungerford & Jackson
446. The rifled musket
447. Memphis Novelty Works
448. 60% or 400,000
449. Six pounder
450. 20-pound Parrot
451. Land mines
452. Griswold and Gunnison of Georgia
453. Nine
454. The Enfield
455. The Napoleon Model 1857, a light 12 pounder
456. The Bormann fuze
457. The two band Enfield rifle
458. Counter battery fire
459. Anti-personnel fire
460. A limber
461. Twelve
462. The Swamp Angel
463. Brig. Gen. George W. Rains
464. Cannon barrels
465. Lt. Col. J.W. Mallory
466. An eight-inch smooth-bore Sea Coast gun
467. Le Place Freres in Paris
468. Gen. Joseph Reid Anderson, owner of the Tredegar Iron Works
469. Georgia pikes
470. .36
471. Artillery ammunition

472. By the pound

473. 3,000 .58-calibre rifles

474. Cook and Brothers

475. Morse carbine

476. Kerr revolver

477. The Harp of Erin

478. Edged weapons

479. Bowie knives

480. Forty

481. Ten

482. The 1853 Pattern

483. Long Tom

484. The carbine

485. The Sharps M1859 or M1863

486. J.H. Dance and Brothers

487. A cannon

488. Junius Archer

489. John R. Baylor

490. Cannon barrels

491. John Gilleland of Athens, Georgia

492. A five-shot revolving gun

493. It was spring-loaded

494. 15,000

495. .62 calibre

496. 40,000

Forts, Prisons and Hospitals

497. Alton Prison

498. Fortress Monroe

499. Fort Marshall

500. Castle Pinckney

501. C.S.A. P.O.W. camps in both Richmond and Petersburg carried this name

502. Libby Prison

503. Camp Sumter

504. John H. Winder

505. Built following the War of 1812 to house Congress

506. Point Lookout, Maryland

507. 40,000

508. Felix Oeser, also known as de la Baume

509. Point Lookout, Maryland

510. Chimborazo

511. None

512. Nashville, Tennessee

513. William T. Sherman

514. Corinth, Missippi

107

515. Twenty-four
516. Maggots
517. John H. Winder
518. Lynchburg
519. Dr. E.A. Craighill
520. John J. Terrell, M.D.
521. Col. Louis T. Wigfall
522. Forts Walker and Beauregard
523. Fort Moultrie
524. Fort Morgan
525. Fort Fisher
526. Fortress Monroe
527. Fort Moultrie and Castle Pinckney
528. The North
529. Forty-eight
530. 4,000
531. Fort Loudon
532. Gen. W.H.C. Whiting
533. Andersonville
534. James Brown McCau, M.D.
535. The Charleston militia

TOTAL WAR

War in the East

536. 33%
537. Shenandoah Valley agriculture
538. Jeb Stuart, C.S.A., and Alfred Pleasonton, U.S.A.
539. Gen. Wade Hampton
540. Balls Bluff
541. Elkhorn Tavern
542. 120 miles by 20 miles
543. Six weeks
544. Brig. Gen. Lewis Armistead
545. Thirteen months
546. Shoes
547. Big Bethel, Virginia
548. 30%
549. 29,000
550. Maj. Gen. "Black Dave" Hunter
551. Cold Harbor
552. First Manassas
553. 15,000
554. To obtain supplies

ANSWERS

555. 64 hours
556. Gaines's Mill, Virginia
557. She lost 8,750 of her 57,000 troops
558. Malvern Hill
559. The Federal supplies at Manassas Junction
560. Gen. Daniel H. Hill
561. Burnside's Bridge
562. Pickett's Charge
563. 292
564. Maj. Gen. H. Judson Kilpatrick
565. Petersburg, Virginia
566. Col. Charles Cummings
567. Wilderness Church
568. Brandy Station, Virginia
569. Northwest
570. Olustee
571. Gen. James Longstreet
572. Gen. William Barksdale
573. U.S. XI Corps
574. Maj. Gen. Henry Heth
575. Lee's Special Order No. 191
576. Gen. John D. Imboden
577. Lee and Gordon's Mill
578. Lower Bridge or Roherback Bridge
579. The Mule Shoe
580. Bentonville, North Carolina
581. Rickett's
582. Gen. Richard Ewell
583. Hatcher's Run
584. Animal unrest: stampeding deer, small animals and birds in flight
585. The Slaughter House
586. Yorktown
587. Shiloh
588. Front Royal, Virginia
589. Cedar Creek
590. Gaines's Mill
591. Roanoke Island, North Carolina
592. Brig. Gen. W.S. Harney
593. The Sherfy family
594. Nearly 23,000
595. Ammunition
596. Stonewall Jackson
597. Greencastle

ANSWERS

598. Battle of Stones River, Tennessee

599. Gettysburg

600. Mid-November 1864

601. Malvern Hill

602. Stones River

603. The Seven Days' Battles

604. Lewis Armistead, James Kemper and Richard Garnett

605. New Hope Church, Dallas, Georgia

606. The Battle of South Mountain

607. Thirty-four hours

608. A powder ship

War in the West

609. Cotton

610. Mexico

611. John Robert Baylor

612. The Choctaws

613. Cumberland Gap

614. Santa Fe, New Mexico

615. Maj. Gen. Patrick R. Cleburne

616. Valverde, New Mexico

617. Four

618. Brig. Gen. Henry H. Sibley

619. He was in Frankfort, Kentucky, attending the swearing-in ceremony of the Confederate governor

620. Gen. John Turchin

621. Murfreesboro

622. 10th Cavalry

623. Nathan B. Forrest

624. Black Kettle

625. All of present-day Arizona and New Mexico and part of Nevada

626. Granville Ovry

627. Mesilla

628. Col. John R. Baylor

629. Valverde, New Mexico

630. Lances

631. David E. Twiggs

632. Sabine Pass, Texas

633. Sabine Pass, Texas

634. Maj. Gen. Leonidas Polk

635. Lt. Gen. Stephen Dill Lee

636. Gen. E. Kirby Smith

637. Gen. John B. Hood

638. Bill Anderson

639. Gen. Joseph Shelby

640. The Wigfall mess

641. Choctaw, Chickasaw, Cherokee, Creek and Seminole

642. Chusto-Talasah, Honey Springs, Oklahoma

643. Gen. Joseph E. Johnston

644. Eleven: five killed, one mortally wounded, five wounded

645. The Alabama House

646. Galveston, Texas

647. Douglas Hancock Cooper

War at Sea

648. Eleven

649. John Newland Maffit

650. Laird Shipyards, Liverpool, England

651. C.S.S. *Atlanta*

652. Japanese

653. C.S.S. *Chicora*

654. "Whistling Dick"

655. U.S.S. *Hatteras*

656. John M. Brooke

657. Ram fever

658. John Randolph Tucker

659. Lt. William T. Glassell

660. Rear Adm. Raphael Semmes

661. Gov. Francis Pickens

662. John Lube Porter

663. Sweeping for mines

664. The *Hunley*

665. C.S.S. *Manassas*

666. Col. Lloyd Bell

667. One in three

668. 25%

669. Lt. William H. Parker

670. The Conf. Naval Academy training ship

671. Capt. John Taylor Wood

672. The C.S.S. *Tallahassee,* then known as the C.S.S. *Olustee*

673. U.S.S. *Keokuk*

674. Four

675. Port Royal, South Carolina

676. C.S.S. *Virginia*

677. C.S.S. *Albemarle*

678. C.S.S. *Arkansas*

ANSWERS

679. *Star of the West*
680. C.S.S. *Huntress*
681. C.S.S. *Hunley*
682. Capt. William H. Parker
683. Brig. Gen. Gabriel J. Rains
684. The *James Gray*
685. Cuba
686. C.S.S. *Teaser*
687. Bermuda or Nassau
688. Matthew Fontaine Maury
689. Lt. Charles W. Read
690. Selma, Alabama
691. C.S.S. *Shenandoah*
692. The *William Aiken*
693. Fourteen
694. On a floating battery
695. Letters of Marque and Reprisal
696. To skip the rounds
697. The *Savannah*
698. Hang Yankee sailors
699. C.S.S. *Sumter*
700. The *Enrica*
701. Because the clucking would give away their position
702. It produced little smoke
703. So it could not be heard
704. Pres. Buchanan did not wish war
705. The U.S.S. *San Jacinto*
706. They sent 8,000 troops to Canada
707. Sixty-four
708. Columbus, Georgia
709. C.S.S. *David*
710. Forty
711. 305
712. Thirty-eight ships and 1,053 prisoners
713. C.S.S. *Alabama*
714. Gray
715. The C.S.S. *North Carolina* and the C.S.S. *Raleigh*

War on Rails

716. The Georgia State and East Tennessee railroads
717. The Richmond & Petersburg
718. Bristoe Station
719. Strategic use of railroads

ANSWERS

720. East Tennessee and Virginia R.R.
721. 8,541 miles
722. The "Fred Leach"
723. The Baltimore and Ohio
724. 113
725. William A. Fuller
726. Seized Southern railroads
727. Coal
728. John W. Garrett
729. Martinsburg, Virginia (now West Virginia)
730. Iron-clad wooden rails
731. Wounded soldiers
732. Five to seven cars
733. 965
734. The Virginia Central

Strategy

735. It was a last attempt to wrest Missouri from Federal control
736. The firing on Fort Sumter
737. Generals A.P. Hill and R.S. Ewell
738. Morgan always operated behind the enemy lines
739. Three
740. 60,000
741. August 19, 1863
742. Washington, D.C.
743. Five
744. Maj. Gen. Braxton Bragg invaded Kentucky
745. Salt and lead
746. William T. Sherman
747. To leave office before war started.
748. The South could not clothe, feed nor arm them
749. Stonewall Jackson
750. Gen. Albert Sidney Johnston
751. Robert E. Lee
752. Two
753. The Peninsular Campaign
754. Maj. Gen. Jubal Early
755. Chancellorsville
756. The Anaconda Plan
757. The Yankee blockade
758. $200,000
759. Hanover Junction, Virginia
760. Gen. Edward Porter

113

ANSWERS

Alexander

761. Holly Springs, Mississippi
762. Hampton
763. Capt. Marcellus M. Moorman
764. Logistics
765. Ringgold and Dyers Bridges
766. Lookout Mountain

Geography

767. Kenesaw, Georgia
768. Washington County, Maryland
769. Apache Canyon, (Santa Fe County, New Mexico)
770. The James
771. Charlotte, North Carolina
772. Warren County
773. The Potomac River
774. The James and the York
775. Strasburg, Virginia
776. Rappahannock River
777. New Orleans (pop. 168,675 in 1860)
778. Indian Creek
779. Guyandotte, Cambell County

780. The Chickahominy
781. The James River
782. White's Ford
783. Baton Rouge, Louisiana
784. Salt
785. The Luray Valley
786. Military headquarters and cemetery
787. Tishomingo Creek
788. Selma
789. New Orleans
790. Red Bud Run
791. The Potomac
792. Vicksburg
793. Indiana and Ohio
794. The Appomattox and the James
795. The North Fork of the Shenandoah
796. Doctor's Creek
797. The Appalachian Mountains
798. Cemetery Ridge, Gettysburg, Pennsylvania
799. Plum Run

ANSWERS

800. Antietam Creek
801. Bull Run
802. Williamsport
803. River of Death
804. Richmond 38,000
805. The Blue Ridge Mountains
806. Willoughby Run
807. Shiloh
808. Harpeth River

THE CAUSE

Politics and Government

809. The Whigs
810. Peaceful Southern separation
811. Robert Brown
812. $2 billion
813. Postmaster General
814. John Brown
815. 106
816. 26
817. Thomas Hill Watts
818. E.C. Elmore
819. $1 billion
820. Stephen Russell Mallory

821. Col. Robert Ould
822. Brig. Gen. Samuel P. Moore
823. February 8, 1861
824. They represented the Confederate Provisional government in England
825. William S. Morris
826. Southern military decorations
827. May 1861
828. John H. Reagan
829. Charlotte, North Carolina (April 26, 1865)
830. It was never dissolved. It adjourned for the last time on March 18, 1865
831. Robert Mercer Taliaferro Hunter
832. 8,411
833. Maj. Gen. John E. Wood
834. The draft
835. 1820s
836. Field frank
837. His signature
838. May 28, 1861
839. A confederacy

115

ANSWERS

840. Caleb Huse
841. Judah P. Benjamin
842. Alexander H. Stephens
843. Abraham Lincoln
844. James M. Calhoun
845. The signers of the Articles of Secession
846. The Willard
847. John Tyler
848. Judah P. Benjamin
849. Chistopher G. Memminger
850. Ulysses S. Grant
851. New York City
852. John J. Crittenden
853. Washington D.C.
854. Henry A. Wise
855. Andrew Jackson
856. John B. Floyd
857. Henri Mercier
858. Zebulon B. Vance
859. Alabama
860. Maryland (September 1861)
861. The Free Soil Party
862. 20% (127,000)
863. Columbia, South Carolina
864. Kentucky
865. New York
866. Richard Yates
867. William Gilpin
868. 38,000
869. Thomas Holliday Hicks
870. New York
871. Washington, D.C.
872. Indiana
873. The hanging of John Brown
874. Illinois
875. Cmdr. James D. Bulloch
876. West Virginia from Virginia
877. Gen. B.F. "Spoons" Butler
878. Maj. Gen. Winfield Scott
879. Joseph Brown of Georgia
880. Maryland
881. John Letcher
882. Florida
883. Virginia
884. Sam Houston
885. Texas, Virginia and Ten-

nessee

886. By blockading Southern ports
887. Secretary of War
888. Joseph Carrington Mayo
889. Francis Pickens

The Homefront

890. Seventy-two
891. 10% per month
892. John C. Frémont and David Hunter
893. Ginger beer
894. Cotton
895. None
896. The *Desire*
897. Virginia
898. Justice Roger Brooke Taney
899. Livestock
900. George W.L. Bickley
901. Montgomery C. Meigs
902. About 6 million
903. Germany
904. Massachusetts (1641)
905. 1862
906. 22 million
907. 1808
908. Georgia
909. Armfield and Harrison
910. Washington, D.C.
911. Treasonous
912. About a quarter million
913. Scottish, Irish or Welsh
914. About 60,000
915. About 133,000
916. $200
917. A ticket to the show "Tableaux and Charades"
918. The Fourth of July
919. About one-third
920. Fireballs
921. About 40%
922. William Jones
923. $68.22
924. First African Church
925. Yellow fever
926. Six percent

Music, Words and Images

927. Jefferson Davis's inaugura-

117

ANSWERS

tion (February 18, 1861)

928. A drummer and a fifer

929. John Hunt Morgan

930. "Maryland, My Maryland"

931. Wright & Bell

932. Petersburg, Virginia

933. Patrick S. Gilmore

934. Marching in step

935. Blind Tom

936. "The Bonnie Blue Flag"

937. Earnest Halphin

938. "The Yellow Rose of Texas"

939. 750

940. "Dixie"

941. James E. Taylor

942. Associated Press

943. Alexander Gardner and Timothy O'Sullivan

944. Carte de visite (CDV)

945. Armstead and Taylor

946. George S. Cook

947. *Frank Leslie's Illustrated News*

948. In New York City, by Southern sympathizers

949. Jefferson Davis

950. Osborn and Durbee

951. Edward Pollard

952. President Lincoln

953. Sam Upham

954. Washington's birthday

955. The Nashville *Banner*

956. Arthur J.L. Fremantle

957. Stonewall Jackson

958. William Lloyd Garrison

959. The *Chicago Tribune*

960. *Harpers Weekly*

961. Edward Pollard

962. The New York *Daily News*

963. The U.S. mail

964. John Esten Cooke

965. Benjamin "Spoons" Butler

966. An information booklet for the capital of the Confederacy

967. J.L.M. Curry

968. John R. Tompson

969. Robert Barnwell Rhett

970. Tap enemy lines

971. Jefferson Davis

972. *The Index*

After Appomattox

973. Apple
974. Brig. Gen. Joshua L. Chamberlain
975. Col. Charles Marshall
976. Ten years
977. Theodore Roosevelt
978. Samuel A. Mudd, M.D.
979. Mary Surratt
980. 1889
981. Joseph Wheeler
982. Confederate Memorial Day
983. Five days
984. Thaddeus Stevens (R-Pennsylvania)
985. American Indians
986. Edwin M. Stanton, Secretary of War
987. *Ex parte* Milligan
988. Reconstruction
989. Joseph E. Johnston
990. Abbeville, South Carolina
991. Alexander Gardner
992. Sen. Charles Sumner (R-Massachusetts)
993. Knights of the White Camelia
994. Three molars
995. Michael Miley
996. 1896
997. John S. Ford
998. Brig. Gen. Stand Watie
999. Felix H. Robertson
1000. March 28, 1959
1001. Brig. Gen. James E. Slaughter

Select Bibliography

Books

Albaugh, William A. III, and Edward N. Simmons. *Confederate Arms*. New York: Bonanza Books, Crown Pub., 1967.
Angle, Paul M. *The Civil War Years*. New York: Doubleday, 1967.
Battles and Leaders of the Civil War. New York: Century Magazine, 1884.
Blackerby, H.C. *Blacks in Blue and Gray*. Tuscaloosa, Ala.: Portals Press, 1979.
Botkin, B.A. *A Civil War Treasury*. New York: Random House, 1960.
Colton, Ray C. *The Civil War in the Western Territories*. Norman, Okla.: University of Oklahoma Press, 1984.
Edwards, William B. *Civil War Guns*. Harrisburg, Pa.: Stackpole, 1962.
Faust, Patricia L., ed. *Historical Times Illustrated Encyclopedia of the Civil War*. New York: Harper & Row, 1986.
Freeman, Douglas Southall. *Lee's Lieutenants, Vols. I-III*. New York: Charles Scribner's & Sons, 1942-1945.
Gavin, William G. *Accoutrement Plates*. York, Pa.: Shumway Pub., 1975.
Gorgas, J. Cole. *The Ordnance Manual*. Dayton, Oh.: Morningside, 1976.
Griffith, Paddy. *Battles in the Civil War*. Camberley, Surrey, England: Fieldbooks, 1986.
Grissom, Michael A. *Southern by the Grace of God*. Gretna, La.: Pelican Publishing Co., 1989.
Johnson, James R. and Alfred H. Bill. *Horsemen Blue and Gray*. New York: Oxford Univ. Press, 1960.
Kane, Harnett T. *Gone are the Days*. New York: Bramhall House, 1960.
Katcher, Philip. *American Civil War Armies (1): Confederate Artillery, Cavalry and Infantry*. London: Osprey Publications, 1986.
Kennedy, James R. and Walter D. Kennedy. *The South was Right*. Baton Rouge: Land & Land Pub., 1991.
Lord, Francis A. *Civil War Collector's Encyclopedia, Vol. I*. Harrisonburg,

Pa.: Stackpole, 1962.

McWhiney, Grady. *Cracker Culture*. Tuscaloosa, Ala.: University of Alabama Press, 1988.

Miller, F.T. *The Photographic History of the Civil War*. New York: Patriot Pub., 1911.

Minor, Charles C. *The Real Lincoln*. Harrisonburg, Va.: Sprinkle Publications, 1992.

Ordance Bureau. *The Field Manual*. Richmond, Va.: Ritchie Y Dunnavant, 1862.

Sifkis, Stewart. *Who Was Who in the Civil War*. New York: Facts on File, 1988.

Stern, Philip Van Doren. *The Confederate Navy*. New York: Bonanza Books, Crown Pub., 1962.

———. *Soldier Life*. New York: Bonanza Books, Crown Pub., 1961.

Symond, Craig L. *A Battlefield Atlas of the Civil War*. Baltimore: Nautical and Aviation Pub., 1962.

Taylor, Walter H. *Four Years with General Lee*. New York: Bonanza Books, Crown Pub., 1962.

Trudeau, Noah Andre. *Bloody Roads South*. Boston: Little Brown & Co., 1989.

Turner, Charles W. *Ted Barclay, Liberty Hall Volunteers: Letters from the Stonewall Brigade*. Natural Bridge Station, Va.: Rockbridge Publishing Co., 1992.

U.S. War Dept. *The War of the Rebellion: Official Records of the Union and Confederate Armies.* Washington: 1880-1901.

Warner, Ezra J. *Generals in Gray*. Baton Rouge, La.: Louisiana State University Press, 1959.

Wiley, Bell I. *Embattled Confederates*. New York: Bonanza Books, Crown Pub., 1964.

Magazines

America's Civil War. Leesburg, Va.: Empire Press. (various issues)

Civil War Magazine. Berryville, Va.: The Civil War Society. (various issues)

Civil War Times Illustrated. Harrisburg, Pa.: Cowles Pub. (various issues)

Confederate Veteran. Houston, Tx.: Sons of Confederate Veterans. (various issues)

North-South Trader's Civil War. Orange, Va.: North-South Trader. (various issues)

Index

Please note that the numbers following each entry are QUESTION NUMBERS, not page numbers.

1st Maryland, C.S.A. 107, 588
1st Maryland, U.S.A. 588
1st North Carolina 390
1st Texas 267, 599
1st Virginia Brigade 245
3rd Colorado Volunteer Cavalry, U.S.A. 624
3rd Texas 312
6th North Carolina 306
6th Virginia 241
7th Tennessee, C.S.A. 249
7th Tennessee, U.S.A. 249
10th Tennessee 199
10th Texas Cavalry 622
XI Corps, U.S.A. 573, 584
17th Alabama 817
26th North Carolina 858
27th Indiana 575
33rd Virginia 138, 566
44th Mississippi 252
69th North Carolina 275
109th Illinois, U.S.A. 254
abatis 368
Abbeville, South Carolina 990
Abingdon, Virginia 91
abolitionists 32, 814
Adams & Deane 435
Alabama 817, 859
Alabama House, The 645
Alabama Volunteer Corps 290
Alexander, E. Porter 136, 310, 369, 760
Alexandria, Virginia 192

Alton Prison (Illinois) 497
ammunition 456, 461, 463, 465, 471, 480, 481, 595
Anaconda Plan 756
Anderson, "Bloody Bill" 638
Anderson, Joseph Reid 52, 468
Anderson, Robert H. 15, 66, 70, 521, 889, 950
Andersonville Prison 503, 508, 533, 991
"Andes" 395
Andrews Raid 716
Annapolis, U.S. Mil. Acad. 669, 682
Antietam Battlefield 768
Antietam Creek 561, 800
Apache Canyon, New Mexico Terr. 769
Appalachian Mountains 797
Appomattox 234, 760, 973-975
Appomattox River 794
Archer, Junius 488
Arizona Territory 627, 628
Arlington House 149, 786, 901
Armfield and Harrison 909
Armistead, Lewis Addison 43, 72, 116, 544, 604
Armstead and Taylor 945
Armstrong, Frank Crawford 69
Army of Northern Virginia 26, 226, 274, 277, 450, 594, 752
Army of Tennessee 278, 363, 364, 643

123

Army of the Allegheny 277
Army of the Cumberland 766
Army of the Mississippi 634
Arnold, Benedict 960
artillery 56, 108, 118, 240, 263-265, 280, 408, 427, 431, 449, 450, 455, 456, 458-460, 462, 465-467, 471, 472, 483, 487, 489-492, 529, 566, 581, 654, 679, 696
Ashby, Turner 44, 107, 137, 423
Ashby's Gap 805
Associated Press 942
Asworth, Georgia 731
Athens, Alabama 620
Athens, Georgia 491
Atlanta Campaign 542
Atlanta, Georgia 844, 919
Baldwin, William E. 71
balloon, observation 136, 411
Balls Bluff, Battle of 540
Baltimore and Ohio R.R. 723, 727, 728
Banks, Nathaniel 636, 860
Bannon, John B. 74
Barksdale, William 68, 230, 572
Barton, Francis S. 210
Baton Rouge, Louisiana 188, 783
battles (see name of battle)
Baylor, John Robert 489, 611, 628
Baylor, William S. H. 119, 138
Beauregard, P.G.T. 66, 70, 95, 126, 231, 343, 749
Beauvoir 144
Beers, Fannie A. 140
Bell, Lloyd 666
Bellona Arsenal 488
belt buckles and plates 289, 290, 294, 305-307
Benavides, Santos 609
Benjamin, Judah P. 34, 841, 848
Bentonville, Battle of 580
Berdet, James G. 871

Bermuda 687
Bermuda Hundred 717, 794
Berryville, Virginia 408
Bickley, George W.L. 900
Big Bethel, Virginia 392, 547
Big Shanty, Georgia 767
Bilharz, Hall & Co. 420
Black Horse Cavalry 246
Black Kettle 624
black patriots 149, 162, 242, 251, 256, 392, 565, 653, 811, 865, 872, 874, 912, 914, 915, 921, 924, 935, 993
Black Republicans 992
Blair House 23
Blimeal, Fr. J. Emerson 199
"Blind Tom" 935
blockade 667, 757, 886
blockade runners 187, 651, 685, 687, 702, 703, 714
blockading zones 674
Bloody Angle 223
Blue Ridge Mountains 805
bomb proofs 378
"Bonnie Blue Flag, The" 936
Booth, John Wilkes 178, 873
Bormann fuze 456
Boswell, James K. 133
Bottany Cross 336
Bowie knives 479
Boyd, Belle 165
Boyle & Gamble 424
Brady, Mathew 943
Bragg, Braxton 62, 92, 117, 229, 237, 619, 719, 733, 744, 765, 766
Brandy Station, Battle of 538, 568
Breckinridge, John C. 45, 48, 87, 253
Brice's Cross Roads, Battle of 555, 787
Bristoe Station, Virginia 718
Brock, Sallie Ann 145

Brooke, John M. 656
Brooks, Preston 184
Brown, Henry 242
Brown, John 32, 178, 814, 873
Brown, Joseph 879
Brown, Robert 811
Brown, Thornberry 409
Buchanan, James 15, 704, 747, 856
buck and ball 425
bucked and gagged 361
Buena Vista (Mexican War) 3
buffalo hunt 611
Buford, John 569
Buie, Mary Ann 171
Bull Run 801
Bulloch, James D. 875
Bunker Hill, (West) Virginia 103
Burnside, Ambrose 181
Burnside's Bridge 561
Burton, James H. 415
Butler, Benjamin F. "Spoons" 4, 170, 200, 608, 783, 877, 965
buttons 284, 288, 290, 295, 304
C.S.S. *Alabama* 650, 655, 700, 707, 711, 713
C.S.S. *Albemarle* 677
C.S.S. *Arkansas* 678
C.S.S. *Atlanta* 651
C.S.S. *Chicora* 653
C.S.S. *Clarence* 689
C.S.S. *David* 659, 709
C.S.S. *Fingal* 651, 701
C.S.S. *Florida* 649
C.S.S. *Gaines* 690
C.S.S. *Hunley* 681
C.S.S. *Huntress* 680
C.S.S. *Manassas* 665
C.S.S. *Morgan* 690
C.S.S. *North Carolina* 715
C.S.S. *Olustee* 672
C.S.S. *Patrick Henry* 670
C.S.S. *Raleigh* 715

C.S.S. *Selma* 690
C.S.S. *Shenandoah* 691, 712
C.S.S. *Stonewall* 652
C.S.S. *Sumter* 699
C.S.S. *Tallahassee* 671, 672
C.S.S. *Teaser* 686
C.S.S. *Tennessee* 690
C.S.S. *Virginia* 676
Calhoun, James M. 844
Calhoun, John C. 212
Camp Sumter 503
Cape Fear, North Carolina 135
Capital of the Confederacy 827, 831
Captain Lightning 384
carbines: cavalry 484; Hall 421; Morse 475; Sharps 422, 485
Carlisle, Thomas 208
carte de visite (CDV) 944
Cary, Constance 148, 152
Cary, Hetty 152, 159
Cary, Jennie 152
Castle Pinckney 500, 527, 535
Castle Thunder 501
casualties 79, 80, 86, 96, 98, 100, 104, 105, 111, 115, 119, 156, 159, 199, 210, 257, 267, 268, 536, 548, 549, 557, 558, 562, 594, 599, 644
Catfish Hotel 169
Catletts Station, Virginia 279
Cattle Raid 539
cavalry 53, 63, 81, 84, 107, 109, 112, 123, 137, 190, 193, 244, 246-248, 258, 261, 269, 271, 273, 274, 281, 341, 385, 457, 484, 538, 576, 609, 622, 623, 624, 639, 738, 743, 763
Cedar Creek, Battle of 386, 37, 589, 795
Cedar Mountain, Battle of 42, 115, 585
Cemetery Ridge 798

Chamberlain, Joshua L. 974
Chambersburg, Pennsylvania 46, 137, 191
Chambliss, John R. 49
Champion's Hill, Battle of 111
Chancellor, Vespasian 190
Chancellorsville, Battle of 21, 41, 133, 567, 573, 584, 755
Chancellorsville, Virginia 754
Charles Town, (West) Virginia 32, 357
Charleston militia 535
Charleston, South Carolina 70, 110, 176, 462, 499, 523, 527, 535
Charleston Harbor 523, 673, 684
Charlotte, North Carolina 771, 829
Charlottesville, Virginia 763
Chattanooga, Tennessee 542, 766
Cheatham, Benjamin F. 236
"Cheer, Boys, Cheer" 929
Chesapeake Bay 506
Chester Gap 805
Chesterfield, Virginia 488
Chicago Tribune, The 959
Chickahominy River 780
Chickamauga, Battle of 346, 577, 994
Chickamauga River 765, 803
Chickasaw Bluffs, Battle of 635
Chicopee Falls, Mass. 434
Chimborazo Hospital 147, 510, 534
Chivington, John 624
Christian family 201
Christiansburg, Virginia 201
church bells 464
Chusto-Talasah, Battle of 642
"City Intelligenzer" 966
civil rights 9, 181, 219, 741, 864, 868, 952, 959, 985, 987
Civil Rights Act of 1866 985

Claiborne Machine Works 490
Cleburne, Patrick 47, 477, 615
clothing (see uniforms &)
Coggin's Point, Virginia 539
Cold Harbor, Battle of 551
Cold Harbor, Virginia 590
Coldstream Guards, H.M.S. 197
color guards 259
Colorado 867
colors 138, 240, 342 (also see flags)
Columbia, South Carolina 417, 863
Columbus, Georgia 708; Mississippi 441
combat & tactics 21, 204, 368-409
Committee on the Conduct of the War 540
communications 206, 310, 319, 369, 375, 384, 387, 406, 407
commutation fee 349
confederacy, definition of 839
Confederate cabinet 813, 817, 818, 822, 828, 829, 841, 848, 849, 856, 875
Confederate embassy 810
Confederate Lighthouse Serv. 660
Confederate Marine Corps 666
Confederate Memorial Day
Confederate mothers 161
Confederate Naval Academy 669, 670, 673
Confederate Navy 820; strength of 710
Confederate Navy Works 708
Congress of the Confederacy 815, 816, 830, 847, 882, 883
conscription 683, 879
constitution, C.S.A. 823
Cook and Brothers 474
Cook, George S. 946

Cooke, John Esten 964
Cooke, Philip St. George 112
Cooper, Douglas H. 641, 647
"coosh" 351
Copperheads 254
Corinth, Mississippi 514, 945
Corps de Belgique 911
Corps of Engineers 260
cotton 609, 894, 899
Craighill, E.A. 519
Crampton's Gap 606
Crawford, Martin 810
Crittenden, John J. 852
Cuba 685
Cubero, U.S. garrison captured 617
Cumberland Gap 613
Cummings, Charles 566
currency 150, 819, 948, 953, 957
Curry, J.L.M. 967
Curtis, George William 960
Dabb's House 20
Daily News, The New York 962
Dallas, Georgia 605
Dance, J.H. and Brothers 436, 486
Darlington Guards 242
"Daughter of the Confederacy" 153
Davis Guard medal 331, 338
Davis, Jefferson 1-15, 62, 92, 155, 195, 209, 211, 632, 695, 698, 748, 854, 873, 927, 949, 961, 971, 982, 990
Davis, Joe 6
Davis, Sam 185
Davis, Varina Howell 144, 154, 162, 684
Davis, Winnie 153
de la Baume 508
de Polignac, Camille Armand Jules Marie 61
decorations (see medals &)

demographics 862, 912, 913
Denver, Colorado 335
desertion 358, 366
Desire, The 896
Devil's Den 799
diplomats 610, 824, 840
Dix, John 870
"Dixie" 927, 932, 940
Doctor's Creek 796
Dodd, David 180
Dorman, Kate 169
Douglas, Henry Kyd 407
draft 349, 834, 865
dragoons 69, 244
Dred Scott Decision 898
dye, butternut 302
Dyers Bridge 765
Early, Jubal 43, 125, 385, 386, 754, 775
East Tennessee and Virginia R.R. 720
East Tennessee R.R. 716
economics 891, 894, 899
"elephant, seeing the" 371
Elkhorn Tavern, Battle of 541
Elliot Grays (6th Virginia) 241
Ellsworth, E. Elmer 183
Ellsworth, George A. 388
Elmore, E.C. 818
Emancipation Proclamation 892, 895
Emmet, Daniel D. 940
Emperor of China's Yacht, The 713
"Empress Eugenia" 154
enlistees refused 748
Enrica, The 700
equipment 280-282, 291, 308-310, 313-319, 386, 618
Estell Hall 8
European Brigade 238
Evans, Augusta Jane 142
Evans, N.G. 375

127

Ewell, Richard Stoddert 101, 582, 737
ex parte Milligan 987
executions 366, 979, 991
Fairfax, Virginia 82
Falling Waters, Battle of 103
"Father of Secession" 175
Fayetteville, North Carolina 414
field frank 836
"Fightin' Joe" 114
fireballs 920
First African Church 924
flags (also see colors, guidons) 139, 151, 152, 326-330, 333-335, 339-341, 343-348, 680, 977
Florida 570, 882
Floyd, John B. 856
fog 405
fog of war 402
food 350, 351, 353, 359, 363, 364, 893
"Foot Cavalry" 785
Forbes, Edwin 947
"Force Bill" 855
Ford, Antonia J. 141, 168
Ford, John S. 997
foreigners 47, 61, 193, 197, 238, 239, 413, 477, 615, 857, 869, 903, 956
Forrest, Bill 623
Forrest, Nathan Bedford 53, 56, 84, 204, 214, 222, 457, 623
Forsyth, John 810
Fort Beauregard 522
Fort Delaware Prison 143, 871
Fort Donelson, Battle of 778
Fort Fisher 172, 367, 525, 532, 608; Angel of 172
Fort Loudon 531
Fort Manassas 69
Fort Marshall 499
Fort Mason 16

Fort McHenry 116
Fort Morgan 524
Fort Moultrie 15, 523, 527, 889
Fort Negley 512
Fort Pulaski 466
Fort Sanders 531
Fort Sumter 15, 511, 521, 529, 530, 607, 661, 736, 748, 856, 946, 950
Fort Walker 522
Fortress Monroe 498, 526
Fougass 428
Fourth of July 918
Fox's Gap 606
Frank Leslie's Illustrated News 947
Frankfort, Ky. 619
Franklin, Battle of 644, 808
Franklin's Crossing 776
Fraser, John & Co. 176
"Fred Leach," The 722
Frederick, Maryland 256, 758
Fredericksburg, Battle of 220, 370, 376, 397, 572, 776
Fredericksburg, Virginia 754
Free Soil Party 861
Fremantle, Arthur 197, 701, 956
Frémont, John C. 219, 892
Front Royal, Virginia 588
Fuller, William A. 725
Furlough and Bounty Act 355
Gaines's Mill, Battle of 136, 556, 557, 590, 781
galvanized Yankees 243
Galveston, Texas 646, 655
gangrene 516
Gardner, Alexander 943, 991
Garnett, Richard 604
Garnett, Robert S. 98
Garrett, John W. 728
Garrison, William Lloyd 958
Gaston, C.A. 387
Gayoso House hotel 623
Gazette, The (New York) 963

Gen. Order No. 9 (Lee) 26
Gen. Order No. 28 (Butler) 170
Feneral," The 725
Georgia 77, 187, 248, 330, 379, 3532, 561, 879, 908
Georgia Armory 419
Georgia pikes 493
Georgia State R.R. 716
Germany 903
Gettysburg, Battle of 30, 68, 257, 346, 391, 398, 449, 544, 546, 548, 569, 571, 574, 576, 593-595, 597, 599, 604, 799, 806
Gettysburg, Pennsylvania 798
Gilleland, John 491
Gilmer, Jeremy F. 110
Gilmore, Harry 191
Gilmore, Patrick S. 933
Gilpin, William 867
ginger beer 893
Gist, States Rights 75
Glassell, William T. 659
Glaze, William & Co. 417
Glorieta Pass, Battle of 769
"God Save the South" 937
Goodwyn, T.J. 863
Gordon, John Brown 67
Gordonsville, Virginia 734
Gould, A. Willis 53
Grafton, (West) Virginia 409
Grant, U. S. 18, 22, 24, 207, 254, 387, 759, 761, 770, 850, 922, 973
"Gray Ghost" 82
Gray, Selina 149
Great Seal of the Confederacy 954
Greeley, Horace 205
Greenbrier 17
Greencastle, Pennsylvania 597
Greenhow, Rose O'Neal 158
Greensboro, Georgia 441
Greenville Military Works 475

Griswold and Gunnison 452
Groveton, Battle of 596
guidons (also see flags) 341
Guiney's Station, Virginia 37
Guyandotte, (West) Virginia 779
H.M.S. *Trent* 705, 706
habeus corpus (see civil rights)
Halphin, Earnest 937
Hampton Legion 276
Hampton, Virginia 762
Hampton, Wade 276, 539
Hancock, Winfield Scott 72
Hanover Junction, Virginia 759
Hardee, William J. 62, 327, 380
Harney, W.S. 592
Harp of Erin 477
Harpers Ferry arsenal 374, 410, 414, 494
Harpers Ferry, (West) Virginia 35, 372, 494, 592, 723
Harpers Weekly 960
Harpeth River 808
Harrisonburg, Virginia 107
Hart, Nancy 157
Hatcher's Run, Battle of 583
haunted farm 357
head log 403
Hell's Half Acre 621
Henry House 156
Henry, Judith 156
Heth, Henry 574
Hicks, Thomas Holliday 869
Hill, Ambrose Powell 104, 258, 285, 737
Hill, Benjamin H. 195
Hill, Daniel Harvey 36, 97, 229, 235, 560
"Hill the Faithful" 195
Hispanics 239
Holly Springs, Mississippi 761
Honey Springs, Oklahoma 642
Hood, John B. 637, 643, 746

129

Hood's Texans 640, 938
Hooker, Joseph 791
Hotchkiss, Jedediah 54, 131
Houston, Sam 884
Howard, O.O. 567
Howitzer Glee Club 264
Hunley, The 664
Hunter, David 46, 550, 892
Hunter, Robert M.T. 831
Huse, Caleb 840
Hyde & Goodrich 293
Hygeia Hotel 498
Illinois 866, 874
Imboden, John D. 113, 576
indemnity demands 191, 758
Index, The 972
Indian Creek 778
Indiana 793, 872
Indians 255, 269, 275, 612, 624, 641, 642, 647, 803, 985, 998
"Infantry Drill Manual" 380
inflation 891, 9161, 923
insignia 288, 290, 300, 304, 307, 324, 325, 336
ironclads 651, 656, 657, 662, 665, 673, 694, 715
Isaacs, S., Campbell & Co. 314
Iverson's Brigade 257
Jackson, Andrew 855, 978
Jackson, James T. 183, 192
Jackson, Stonewall 20, 31-42, 54, 133, 206, 256, 407, 567, 573, 584, 596, 728, 729, 740, 749, 755, 785, 873, 957, 964
James Gray, The 684
James River 686, 770, 774, 781, 794
Japan 652
"Jeff Davis" 17
"Jeff Davis's pet" 117
Jefferson boots 292
Jefferson, Thomas 13, 102

Jews 850
Jobe, D.S. 182
John Brown's raid 178
Johnson, Andrew 986
Johnson, George W. 174
Johnson, William P. 228
Johnston, Albert Sidney 86, 750, 887
Johnston, Joseph E. 89, 100, 106, 118, 221, 605, 643, 749, 989
Jones, William 922
Jonesboro, Georgia 199, 542
Kemper, James Lawson 604
Kenesaw, Georgia 767
Kennedy, Robert Cobb 173
Kentucky 85, 174, 339, 864
Kentucky invaded 744
Kilpatrick, H. Judson 564
King, J.A. 316
Kirkland, Richard 370
Knights of the Golden Circle 900, 911
Knights of the White Camelia 993
Knobeloch, Margaret Anna Parker 143
Knoxville, Tennessee 531
Ladies Relief Hospital 518
Lady Davis, The 684
Laird Shipyards 650
Lamb, Daisy Chaffee 172
lances 630
land mines (see mines, land and torpedoes)
Lanier, Sidney 187
Latané, William 198
Laurel Brigade 324
Le Place Frères (Paris) 467
Lee and Gordon's Mill 577
Lee, Fitzhugh 64
Lee, Mrs. Robert E. 164
Lee, Phillip Lightfoot 216
Lee, Robert E. 16-30, 39, 51, 65,

73, 108, 149, 203, 207, 218, 220, 224, 227, 232, 234, 329, 387, 391, 568, 571, 576, 581, 583, 737, 743, 744, 751, 752, 754, 755, 760, 782, 802, 837, 854, 873, 901, 930, 960, 973, 975, 983, 995
Lee, Stephen Dill 109, 635
Lee-Custis estate 786
Leech and Rigdon 447, 441, 478
legislators arrested 860
Letcher, John 881
Letters of Marque and Reprisal 695
Lexington, Kentucky 91
Lexington, Virginia 39
Libby Prison 502
Liberia 233
Light Division 258
Limber, Jim 162
Limerick, Ireland 284
Lincoln, Abraham 87, 202, 215, 233, 395, 843, 868, 877, 880, 886, 932, 952, 959, 978, 983, 987
Little Rock, Arkansas 59, 180
Liverpool, England 650
livestock 899
"Long Kentucky Line" 750
"Long Tom" 483
Longstreet, James 51, 60, 83, 99, 207, 364, 571, 993
Longstreet's Corps 364, 733
Lookout Mountain 766
Lorenz 418
Louisiana 130, 304
Lower Bridge 578
"Lucy Long" 28
Luray Valley 785
Lynchburg, Virginia 518, 520
Lyons, Lord 869
Lytle, A.D. 188
Macaria 142
Macon County Volunteers 187

Macon, Georgia 272
Maffit, John Newland 649
maggots 516
Magruder, John 88, 382, 390, 586, 646, 762
Mallory, J.W. 465
Mallory, Stephen R. 820, 875
Malvern Hill, Battle of 558, 601
Manassas, 1st Battle of 90, 156, 210, 221, 246, 310, 375, 440, 483, 545, 552, 566, 581, 749, 753, 801
Manassas Gap 805
Manassas, 2nd Battle of 138, 545, 559, 742, 801
Mann, Ambrose Dudley 824
marching 381, 389, 934
Marine Corps, Conf. 288
Marion Rangers 179
Marmaduke, John 59
Marschall, Nicola 139
Marshall, Charles 975
Marshall House 192
Marshall, John 186
martial law 880
Martinsburg, (West) Virginia 165, 729
Marye's Heights 376
Marye's Heights, Angel of 370
Maryland 134, 336, 337, 860, 869, 880
Maryland, invasion of 744, 782, 930
"Maryland, My Maryland" 930
Mason, James 705
Masons (fraternal order) 66, 68, 72
Massachusetts 184, 896, 904
Maury, Matthew Fontaine 688
Maynard, Edward 412
Mayo, Joseph Carrington 888
McCau, James Brown 534
McCausland, John 46, 191

131

McClanahan, John 113
McClellan, George B. 25, 88, 89, 198, 440, 676, 73, 781
McElroy and Company 478
McGuire, Hunter 41
McLean, Wilmer 194
McPherson Farm 574
medals & decorations 321, 322, 331, 633, 826
Medical Corps/Dept. 283, 316, 515, 822
Meigs, Montgomery C. 124, 901
Memminger, Christopher G. 849
Memories 140
Memphis Novelty Works 447
Memphis, Tennessee 445, 555, 623
Mercier, Henri 857
Mercury, The Charleston 969
Mesilla, New Mexico Terr. 627
Metairie Cemetery 11
Mexican War 3
Mexico 609, 610
Miles, George H. 937
Miley, Michael 995
Milledgeville, Georgia 419
mines, land (also see torpedoes) 428, 451
mines, lead 745
mines, salt 745
Missionary Ridge, Battle of 373
Mississippi 144, 230, 325, 334, 572, 994
Mississippi Nightingales 160, 170
Mississippi River 792
Missouri 179, 339, 735
Mitchell, B.W. 575
Mobile, Alabama 239, 316, 685
Mobile Bay 524
Montgomery, Alabama 8, 151, 827, 831
Moon, Lottie 155

Moore, Samuel P. 822
Moorman, Marcellus M. 763
Morgan, John Hunt 85, 91, 166, 204, 384, 388, 738, 793, 929
Morris, William S. 825
Morton, John W. 56
Mosby, Charles F. 241
Mosby, John Singleton 63, 73, 78, 82, 123, 141, 247, 408
Mosby's Rangers 247
mottoes 323, 332, 622
Mudd, Samuel A. 978
Mule Shoe, The 579
mules 124
Mumford, William 200
Murphreesboro, Battle of 48, 252, 602, 621
musketoon, Navy 495
Myer, Albert J. 369
Nashville *Banner*, The 955
Nashville Military Academy 93
Nashville Plow Works 478
Nashville, Tennessee 490, 512, 637
Nassau, Bahamas 687
national treasury, C.S.A. 990
"nausea" 363
naval base, Northern 675
Naval Yard, C.S.A. 771
New Hope Church, Battle of 605
New Market, Battle of 250, 253
New Mexico, Terr. of 611, 617, 618, 625, 629, 630
New Orleans, Louisiana 170, 200, 238, 240, 293, 413, 685, 777, 789, 965, 993
New York City 173, 851, 865, 870, 948
newspapers/reporting 942, 947, 952, 955, 958-960, 962, 963, 969, 972
nicknames 33, 51, 82, 94, 114, 117,

153, 175, 195, 615
No. 290 700
Norfolk Navy Yard 648
North Carolina 257, 275, 286, 306, 346, 347, 858, 862
O'Sullivan, Timothy 943
Oeser, Felix 508
Ohio 793
Old Capitol prison 141, 168, 505
Old Crow whiskey 125
"Old War Horse" 51
Olustee, Battle of 570
"On to Richmond" 526
Orange and Alexandria R.R. 722
Order of American Knights 911
Osborn and Durbee 950
Ould, Robert 821
Overton home 637
Ovry, Granville 626
palisade 404
Palmetto musket 417
Parker, William H. 669, 682
Partisan Rangers 63, 247
pass box 471
Pea Ridge, Battle of 541, 647
peace commissioners 853
peach orchard 593
Pegram, John 58, 159
Pember, Phoebe Yates 147
Pemberton, John C. 57, 132
Pendleton, William N. 108
Peninsula Army, U.S.A. 558
Peninsula of Virginia 774, 780
Peninsular Campaign 88, 164, 382, 603, 753
Pennsylvania Bucktails 107
Pennsylvania, invasion of 101
Perrin, Abner 223
Perry-Mosher, Kate E. 167
Perryville, Battle of 619, 634, 796
Petersburg, Battle of 563, 565
Petersburg Home Guard 273

Petersburg, Virginia 273, 501, 554, 932
Pettigrew, James J. 103
Philadelphia, Pennsylvania 132
Phillip's Georgia Legion 248
photography 188, 943-946, 950, 991, 995
Pickens, Francis 661, 889
pickets 350, 362
Pickett, George E. 65, 553, 604
Pickett's Charge 270, 398, 544, 562
Pike, Albert 269, 641
pikes 469
Pilot Knob, Battle of 735
pirates 698
Pittsburgh Landing, Battle of 514
Pittsylvania Court House, Virginia 420
Plaquemine Bend 789
Pleasonton, Alfred 538
Plum Run 799
Plymouth, North Carolina 677
poetry 968
Point Lookout, Maryland 509
Point Lookout Prison 187, 506
political parties & movements 75, 809, 861, 992
Polk, Leonidas 50, 236, 634
Pollard, Edward 951, 961
pommeling 429
pontoon bridges 572
Pope, John 279, 297
population 777, 804, 902, 903, 906, 914, 915, 921
Port Hudson, Louisiana 784
Port Royal, South Carolina 522, 675, 751
Porter, John Lube 662
postal service 832, 834, 836-838, 963, 971
Potomac River 506, 581, 773, 782, 791, 802

133

P.O.W. camps 167, 497, 501, 504, 506, 509, 528
prisoners of war 96, 243, 513, 517, 821
prisoners, political 507
Private History of a Campaign that Failed 179
privateers 664, 695, 697, 698
Pulaski, Tennessee 185
Pumpkin Vine Creek 605
punishments 360, 361
Purcell's Battery 265
Quaker guns 440
Quantrill, William 638
Quintero, Joseph A. 610
railroad tracks, miles of 721
railroads, numbers of 724
Rains, Gabriel James 55, 683
Rains, George W. 463
Rains, James E. 105
ram fever 657
Randolph, George W. 102
ranks & titles 123, 127, 128, 134, 146, 261, 263, 519
Rappahannock River 776, 934
Read, Charles W. 689
Ready, Martha 166
Reagan, John H. 813, 828
Rebel yell 552
Reconstruction 976, 984, 988, 992
Red Bud Run 790
Red River Campaign 636
regimental losses 268
regimental organization 259, 262, 266, 383
Reneau, Sally 170
resignations, U.S. military 16, 69, 83, 90, 122, 415, 631, 668
Revolutionary War 296
revolvers: Kerr 476; LeMat 413
rewards 2, 358
Rhett, Robert Barnwell 175, 969

Richardson, Samuel 312
Richmond Armory 416, 495
Richmond arsenal 496
Richmond During the War 145
Richmond Examiner, The 961
Richmond Howitzers 264
Richmond & Petersburg R.R. 717
Richmond, Virginia 6, 14, 19, 20, 49, 58, 89, 91, 99, 146, 148, 154, 297, 422, 424, 430, 495, 501, 502, 510, 551, 734, 804, 827, 831, 834, 888, 903, 924
Rickens, Lucy Holcomb 150
Ricketts's Battery 581
rifle, Enfield 432, 454, 457
rifle, Springfield 454
rifled musket 446, 453, 480; Austrian 418; Enfield 432
Ringgold Bridge 765
Rise and Fall of the Confederate Government, The 949
River of Death 803
Roanoake Island, Battle of 591
Robertson, Felix H. 127, 999
Robertson Hospital 146
Robinson, South Carolina Co. 422
Rock Island, Illinois 167
Roherback Bridge 578
Roll of Honor 826
Roman, Alfred 810
Roosevelt, Theodore 224, 977
Rost, Pierre A. 824
Round Forest 621
roundabout 301
Ruffin, Edmund 196
saber, Pattern 482
Sabine Pass, Battle of 632, 633
Sabine Pass, Texas 169
saddles 280, 282
salaries 354
salt 784
San Juan Hill, Battle of 981

Santa Fe, New Mexico 614
sardine can 289
Savannah, The 697
Sayler's Creek, Battle of 65, 536, 582, 658
scalping 647
Scott, Winfield 878
secession 209, 216, 835, 848, 878, 884, 885
Secession, Articles of 845
Selma, Alabama 690, 788
Semmes, Raphael 134, 660, 699
Seven Days' Battles 601, 603
Seven Pines, Battle of 100, 106
Sharpe, Pvt. — 390
Sharpsburg, Battle of 108, 267, 379, 560, 578, 581, 743, 800
sharpshooters 401, 799
Shelby, Joseph 639
shell jackets 311
Shenandoah River, North Fork 795
Shenandoah Valley 537, 550, 589, 739, 773, 941
Sherfy family 593
Sheridan, Philip H. 589
Sherman, William Tecumseh 126, 213, 222, 513, 600, 746, 845, 863, 989
Shields, Jeff 38
Shiloh, Battle of 86, 126, 174, 228, 513, 587
Shiloh, Mississippi 807
ships (see C.S.S. or U.S.S.)
Shipp, Scott 250
Sibley, Henry H. 318, 614, 618
sick roll 352
sidearms 439; Adams 434
Signal Corps 319
Silent Battle 590
skirmishers 401
Slaughter House 585

Slaughter, James E. 1001
slavery 186, 211, 233, 861, 892, 895-898, 904, 905, 907-910, 912, 922, 924, 926
Slidell, John 705
Smith, Edmund Kirby 93, 636
Smith, Thomas B. 96
Smithfield, (West) Virginia 357
snake buckles 294
Snicker's Gap 805
snipers 401, 433
songs, number written 939
Sons of Confederate Veterans 996
Sons of Liberty 189, 911
South Carolina 71, 75, 175, 184, 242, 307, 468, 661, 679, 845, 889
South Mountain, Battle of 606
Southern Cross of Honor 322
Southern History of the War 951
Southern Telegraph Co. 825
Spanish Guards 239
Special Order No. 191 (Lee) 575
spies 137, 141, 155, 157, 158, 165, 168, 177, 180, 182, 185, 188, 190
Spiller and Burr 442
Spotswood Hotel 14
Spotsylvania, Battle of 223, 579
Spotsylvania, Virginia 759
Spring Hill, Tennessee 129
St. James' church 201
St. Paul's church 58
Stanton, Edwin M. 217, 833, 986
starvation parties 148
Stephens, Alexander H. 842
Stevens, Thaddeus 984
Stevenson, Alabama 645
Stones River, Battle of 236, 598, 602
Stones River, Tennessee 105
Stonewall Brigade 119, 138, 245, 737
"Stonewall Jackson of the West"

615
Stoughton, Edwin Henry 82
Strasburg, Virginia 775
Street, Hungerford & Jackson 445
Stuart, J.E.B. 81, 112, 124, 141, 168, 190, 193, 198, 246, 276, 279, 538, 568, 743, 763, 791
Sturgis, S.D. 555
submarines 659, 664, 681
Sullivan's Island, South Carolina 499
Sumner, Charles 184, 992
Surratt, Mary 979
surrender 22, 203, 207, 983
surrender, last general to 998
sutlers 365
"Swamp Angel" 462
"Swamp Fox of the Confederacy" 94
symbols 337
Tableaux and Charades 917
tactics vs. logistics 764
Tait, P. 284
Taney, Roger Brooke 186, 898
Tappey and Lumsden 492
tariff laws 855
Taylor, James E. 941
Taylor, Richard 130
Taylor, Zachary 130
telegraph 124, 387, 388, 394, 395, 825, 970
Tennessee 613, 885
Tennessee, Dept. of 850
Tennessee, invasion of 746
terms of enlistment 356
Terrell, John J. 520
Texas 16, 113, 127, 269, 325, 436, 631, 632, 884, 885, 887
Texas Lancers 616
Texas Rangers 997
"Texas," The 725
Texas troops 630

Thalian Hall 367
Thermopylae of the Civil War 632
Thomas, George H. 142
Thomas, William Holland 255
Thomas's Highland Legion 255
Thompson, Meriwether 94
Three Months in the Southern States: April-June '63 956
Tidball, John 382
Tilghman, Lloyd 111
Tishomingo Creek 787
Tishomingo Hotel 514
Todd, George 215
"Tom Fool" 33
Tompkins, Sally L. 146
Tompson, John R. 968
Toombs, Robert 379, 561, 578
Torpedo Service 683
torpedoes 55, 663, 688 (also see mines)
Tranter pistol 443
"Traveller" 17, 29, 995
treason, in U.S. Army 833
treasonous organizations 911
Tredegar Iron Works 52, 430, 468
Trenholm, George A. 176
Trent Affair 705, 706
troop strength 270, 553
truce 400
Tucker, John Randolph 658
Tucson, Az. 626
Turchin, John 620
Turner's Gap 606
Twain, Mark 179
Twiggs, David E. 631
Tyler, John 151, 847
Tyler, Letitia 151
Tyler Ordnance Works 473
Tyler, Texas 473
U-rails 730
U.S. constitution 958

136

U.S. Military Academy 52
U.S. Military Railroad 726
U.S.S. *Cincinnati* 654
U.S.S. *Commodore Jones* 663
U.S.S. *Hatteras* 655
U.S.S. *Housatonic* 664
U.S.S. *Keokuk* 673
U.S.S. *Merrimack* 662
U.S.S. *Michigan* 177
U.S.S. *New Ironsides* 659
U.S.S. *San Jacinto* 705
U.S.S. *Star of the West* 661, 679, 704
U.S.S. *William Aiken* 692
uniforms & clothing 31, 40, 279, 283-290, 292, 294-307, 311-313, 320, 546, 748
Union Mills, Virginia 722
Uniontown, Alabama 917
United Confederate Veterans 980
units, organization of 271, 274
Upham, Sam 953
Vallandigham, Clement L. 181, 189
Valley Campaign 385, 740
Valley of Virginia 46
Valverde, Battle of 616, 629
Van Dorn, Earl 129, 761
Vance, Zebulon B. 858
veteran, last Confederate to die 1000
Vicksburg, Battle of 391, 543, 549, 678, 772
Vicksburg Campaign 761
Vicksburg, Mississippi 5, 792, 945
Virginia 435, 881, 883, 885, 897, 914
Virginia Central R.R. 734
Virginia Military Institute 32, 33, 250, 253, 393, 550
von Borcke, Heros 193
Waco, Texas 999

Wade-Davis Bill 988
Walker, Reuben L. 76
Walker, William H.T. 77
Waller, Lucius 59
Wallingford & Murphy 335
war debt 812
War of 1812 116
Warren County, Mississippi 772
Washington Artillery 240
Washington College 39
Washington County, Maryland 768
Washington, D.C. 23, 505, 742, 810, 846, 853, 871, 905, 910
Watie, Stand 998
Watson, A.A. 202
Watts, Thomas Hill 817
weapons 42, 55, 106, 118, 252, 293, 410-496, 603, 630, 698
Welch, O.G. 269
Wells, Gideon 225
West Point 43, 70, 77, 95, 121
West Virginia, secession of 876
Wheeler, Joseph 114, 981
"When Johnny Comes Marching Home" 933
Whigs 809
"Whistling Dick" 654
White House of the Confederacy 14, 811
White House (Washington, D.C.) 24
White's Ford 782
White's Tavern, Virginia 49
Whiting, W.H.C. 135, 532
Whitney, The 442
Whittier, Charles A. 226
Whitworth 431, 433
Wigfall, Louis T. 521
Wigfall mess 640
Wilderness, Battle of the 60
Wilderness church 567

137

Wilkes, Charles 705
Willard Hotel 846
Williams, Walter Washington 1000
Williamson, William 662
Williamsport, Maryland 802
Willoughby Run 806
Wilmington Ladies' Soldiers Aid Society 171
Wilmington, North Carolina 202, 367, 715, 925
Winchester, 3rd Battle of 790
Winchester, Virginia 382, 890
Winder, Charles S. 115
Winder, John H. 504, 517
Windsor, New York 131
Winthrop, Theodore 392
Wirz, Heinrich H. 508, 533, 991
Wise, Henry A. 854
Wizard Clipp 357
Woman Order 170
Wood, John E. 833
Wood, John Taylor 671
Wright & Bell 931
Wythe Rifles 392
Xerxes 221
XI Corps, U.S.A. 573, 584
Yale University 841
Yancey, William Lowndes 824
Yates, John Bell 177
Yates, Richard 866
yellow fever 925
"Yellow Rose of Texas, The" 938
Yokohama, Japan 672
York River 774
Yorktown, Battle of 89, 451
Yorktown, Virginia 586
Ziegler's Grove 798
Zollicoffer, Felix Kirk 955
Zouaves 500, 941

About the Author

In the summer of 1945, young John Hightower purchased his first cavalry sabre for 75 cents in a transaction financed by his father. It was his introduction to what has become a lifetime of buying, selling, swapping and studying the relics of the War for Southern Independence — edged weapons, firearms, buttons, belt plates, accoutrements and photographs.

Hightower was the charter Commander of the Turner Ashby Camp #1567 of the Sons of Confederate Veterans in Winchester, Va., and served as aide-de-camp to past Commander-in-Chief William D. Hogan. He is currently Commander of the 4th Virginia Brigade and Chief of Staff of the Army of Northern Virginia.

Hightower is also belongs to the Company of Military Historians, the National Rifle Association, the Military Order of the Stars and Bars and is a member of the Alabama Masonic Lodge of Military Research. His work has been published in more than a dozen magazines.

Hightower and his wife make their home in the Shenandoah Valley, where he is Advertising Director for *Civil War* magazine.

THE CONFEDERATE CHALLENGE Accepts Your Challenge!

Ooops! If you find a substantive error lurking amid these 1,001 fascinating facts, tell us! Use this form or a copy of it to mail or fax your correction to John M. Hightower, and cite your source(s) in detail so our researchers may verify. If your correction is confirmed and was the first to reach us, you'll get an autographed copy of THE CHALLENGE and credit in the next (corrected) edition. —THE PUBLISHERS

Okay, CHALLENGE, I challenge your facts in Question #_____

Instead of _____

_____

_____ ,

it should be _____

_____

_____ ,

according to _____

_____ .

(Need more room? Use another sheet. Only one question per page, please.)

Name _____

Address _____

City _____ , State ____ Zip _____

Mail to: John M. Hightower
c/o Rockbridge Publishing Co.
P.O. Box 70-B, Natural Bridge Station, VA 24579
Or fax to: (703) 291-1346

Phone (703) 291-1063
All corrections must be submitted in writing. Thank you!

Looking ahead to 1993 . . .

Major General James Lawson Kemper, C.S.A.: VIRGINIA'S FORGOTTEN SON
by Harold Woodward, Jr.   (April 1993) hardcover; price to be set
From the halls of the state legislature to the field of combat as an officer in the Confederate Army and finally as governor of Virginia, James Lawson Kemper dedicated the bigger part of his life to serving his home state of Virginia, but until Harold Woodward, Jr., undertook this biography, Kemper truly seemed to be forgotten. A fascinating look at the man and his times. Photographs. ISBN 0-9623572-7-8

COUNTRY ROADS: ALBEMARLE COUNTY, VIRGINIA
by Susan De Alba   (April 1993) trade paper; $16.95
Visitors come to Charlottesville/Albemarle to see the University of Virginia and Thomas Jefferson's home at Monticello. This collection of driving tours guides visitors to these popular places and much, much more. Follow old Indian trails that became planked highways and are now delightful byways through mountain passes and across fertile plains. Explore the James River Road and end up on "Walton's Mountain." Each tour has its own map and easy instructions. ISBN 0-9623572-1-9

Send for a **free catalog:** ROCKBRIDGE PUBLISHING COMPANY, P.O. Box 70-B, Natural Bridge Station, VA 24579

Name _____

Address _____

City_____ State_____ Zip_____

I'm especially interested in books about _____
_____
_____
_____

Also from Rockbridge Publishing Company...

_____ **Ted Barclay, Liberty Hall Volunteers: LETTERS FROM THE STONEWALL BRIGADE**
by Charles W. Turner, editor hardcover $19.95
Four years of war recorded by a well-educated young Virginian who lauds Southern leaders and laments the realities of the battlefield in vivid prose. Includes 140 photos and mini-biographies of about 200 comrades and civilians. ISBN 0-9623572-4-3

_____ **LEXINGTON IN OLD VIRGINIA**
by Henry Boley trade paper; reprint $16.95
With photographs by Michael Miley, who was known as Gen. Lee's photographer. Nine chapters relate to the Civil War. Personal reflections and stories of fellow townspeople include town history, Virginia Military Academy, Washington and Lee University, told in an intimate, charming style. ISBN 0-9623572-2-7

_____ **GLASGOW, VIRGINIA: 100 YEARS OF DREAMS**
by Lynda Mundy-Norris Miller hardcover $35.00
Photographs and memories tell the story of "boom towns" all over the Valley of Virginia. At the confluence of the James and Maury rivers, Glasgow was a prime target for high-talking 1890s land developers who quickly faded away, leaving the sturdy Scotch-Irish settlers to turn their own dreams into reality. ISBN 0-9623572-5-1

_____ **COUNTRY ROADS: ROCKBRIDGE COUNTY, VIRGINIA**
by Katherine Tennery and Shirley Scott paper. wirebound $12.95
Tour the back roads near historic Lexington. Detailed maps guide you past manor houses, log cabins, Victorian villages, the soaring Natural Bridge and much, much more! Easy-to-read history for armchair travelers and delightful day trips for visitors. ISBN 0-9623572-0-0

_____ **LEXINGTON, VIRGINIA: A RIDE IN THE COUNTRY**
adapted by Katherine Tennery audiocassette $9.95
Based on the Country Roads guidebook, this spritely narrative offers country roads an ordinary tourist would never find, roads that follow Indian paths and roads used by Gen. Lee when he roamed the countryside with his faithful Traveller. A half-day tour, longer if you linger at one or more points of interest.

Order from your favorite bookstore or directly from **Rockbridge Publishing Co., P.O. Box 70-B, Natural Bridge Station, VA 24579.** Please add 4.5% sales tax in Virginia. For shipping & handling, include $2.50 for first book or tape, $1 each additional item to same address. Ask for a free catalog!